LOSS OF THE SELF

In Modern Literature and Art

BOOKS BY WYLIE SYPHER

Enlightened England

Four Stages of Renaissance Style:
Transformations in Art and Literature, 1400-1700

Guinea's Captive Kings

Rococo to Cubism in Art and Literature

Loss of the Self: In Modern Literature and Art

LOSS OF THE SELF
in modern literature and art

WYLIE SYPHER

Random House, New York

ACKNOWLEDGMENTS

I must first express what I owe to the editorial staff at Random House, especially to Jason Epstein and Andrew Chiappe, both of whom have given their attention to this manuscript, as well as to Evelyn Kossoff, whose skill and intelligence have improved these pages. I am also indebted to the University of Virginia and The National Gallery of Art for allowing me to adapt certain passages from lectures given at these institutions.

It is especially pleasing to mention the courtesy and good will of Jean Dubuffet in permitting me to reprint passages from his indispensable lecture on "Anticultural Positions" given at The Arts Club of Chicago in December, 1951; and The Arts Club has been equally gracious in consenting to my use of this lecture. The text of the lecture itself has been checked by Peter Selz, Curator of The Museum of Modern Art in New York, whose generosity I appreciate.

For permission to quote from copyrighted material, I am indebted to the following:

Harry N. Abrams, Inc. for a passage from *Art Since 1945*, edited by Marcel Brion

George Allen and Unwin, Ltd. and The Macmillan Company for passages from Robert Linssen's *Living Zen*, translated by Diana Abrahams-Curiel, 1958

City Lights Books for a passage from Allen Ginsberg's *Howl*. Copyright 1956 by Allen Ginsberg.

Grove Press, Inc. for passages from Samuel Beckett's *The Unnamable*, copyright 1958; from *Molloy*, copyright 1955; from Eugène Ionesco's *Victims of Duty*, copyright 1958; from Alain Robbe-Grillet's "A Fresh Start for Fiction," translated by Richard Howard, *Evergreen Review*, no. 3, copyright 1957; and from Henry Miller's *Tropic of Capricorn*

Harcourt, Brace and World, Inc. for a passage from T. S. Eliot's "Burnt Norton" in *Four Quartets*

Alfred A. Knopf, Inc. for a passage from Wallace Stevens' "So-and-So Reclining on Her Couch." Copyright 1947, 1954 by

Wallace Stevens. Reprinted from the *Collected Poems of Wallace Stevens*.

Martin Secker and Warburg Ltd. for passages from Robert Musil's *The Man Without Qualities*

The Viking Press Inc. for a passage from Jack Kerouac's *On The Road*

Wayne State University Press for passages from Robert Musil's *The Man Without Qualities*

Auburndale, Massachusetts
September, 1961

For L. J. S.

Contents

"L'homme n'est plus, s'il l'a jamais été,
le seul héros"—Pierre Volboudt in
Les Assemblages de Jean Dubuffet

This book originated as one of the lectures given in the Peters Rushton Seminars at the University of Virginia, and I am grateful to the University for allowing me to adapt some of these pages. As I was preparing this lecture, I found that there was an indefinable fringe of material I could not get into it, and also that I wanted to say something more about the recent literature and painting touched upon in the last chapter of my *Rococo to Cubism*. Then after I read Claude Mauriac's *The New Literature*, a good many things seemed to fall together. In a sense my remarks are only an extension of Mauriac's chapters, and my reliance on Mauriac will be only too clear to those who know his book. While I was reading Mauriac, I happened to come upon a number of articles devoted to the strange painting done by Jean Dubuffet, along with the stimulating discussion of modern art in Jean Grenier's *Essais sur la Peinture Contemporaine*. These essays confirmed and supplemented what Mauriac had said, and I have used them at every turn.

The coincidence seemed all the happier when Frank De Sua called my attention to certain recent developments in mathematical theory, notably the examination of the premises of mathematics made by Kurt Goedel, whose speculations I cannot, of course, follow in any detail. Yet I thought I saw a relation between Goedel's main conclusions, which are intelligible even to a novice, and certain tendencies in the novel, in the theater, in painting. This relation appears more striking if one considers some of the statements made by scientists like Werner Heisenberg, Erwin Schroedinger, Percy Bridgman, and Michael Polanyi. Again, it would be presumptuous to imply that I understand the work of these scientists in any depth; but I have followed J. Bronowski's explanation in *The Common Sense of Science*, and it should be possible for a layman to gather in what direction they are moving and the relevance of these theories to the arts of the day. Finally, I am sure that specialists in phenomenology, general semantics, and symbolic logic will already have gone so far beyond me that what I venture to say may seem to be not only superficial but reckless.

Howbeit I believe Werner Heisenberg is justified in stating in *Physics and Philosophy* that there is some reciprocity between what scientists are thinking and what artists are doing. In accepting the notion of this reciprocity Heisenberg is emphasizing what Gertrude Stein was fond of proposing: that the truly significant art is, and must be, "contemporary" art exactly because the artist is one who senses as quickly and strongly as the scientist or philosopher which way the deeper currents of his day are running. There are always cross currents, to be sure, but even these countercurrents will somehow be expressed in the science, in the philosophy, in the novel, drama, or painting and poetry that is truly contemporary. The problem seems to me not to try to define

4

"the spirit of the time," which too easily leads us toward a mystique, but instead simply to note what equivalences, correspondences, interactions can be found between what is happening in the arts, in literature, in science and philosophy. I should hope that if some of these correspondences or equivalences can be suggested we can respond better to recent literature and painting, which then should "mean" more than they otherwise might.

It is probably useless to try to guard one's self against misinterpretation, for one will be judged anyhow by what one is thought to have said. But if I can, I should like to prevent two misconceptions of what I am trying to do. The first misconception would be that I have presumed the artist—the painter, novelist, or dramatist—to have studied for himself the science of our day or to have read Heisenberg or Schroedinger. A few may have done so; but surely most have not. Yet these artists often are working along with scientists, in the same direction, even if they may not know they are doing so; and they are likely to be as sensitive as scientists to what is really contemporary. If one is an artist, one does not need schooling to respond to the turn of our interests.

A second misconception would be that I am approving or disapproving what is now being written or painted, or that I am defending or attacking modern art. Modern art is simply there, and I am only recognizing that it exists. I am chiefly concerned to explain, as far as I can do so, what it "means." To be sure, I like Beckett better than I like Fautrier—in fact, I wonder if Fautrier will survive long as a painter, and I suspect Beckett may survive quite a while as novelist. It is impossible to disguise preferences, and I have not tried to do so very carefully; but often the artists one likes least are those who prove to be most indicative, important, or even exciting when one asks what is distinctively modern about their work. Consequently I have spoken at length about some writers and painters I do not greatly like but find highly illustrative. The real danger, of course, is in losing perspective when one discusses the contemporary arts, and perhaps we should all keep in mind James Thurber's remark on the moderns generally: "How long can the needle of the human gramophone stay in the rut of *Angst* without wearing out and ending in the repetition of a ghoulish gibbering?"

All this is neither defense nor apology. No apology is needed for attempting to interpret the contemporary arts; and these pages are intended as commentary, not as large-scale treatment aiming at completeness. Too many revisions must be made before any such treatment is possible; and they will be made by somebody else.

A word about the commentary itself: I have tried to bring into contrast the "romantic" self of the nineteenth century and the self in our own day, which I have called an anonymous self. Here also I have been anticipated by Robert Greer Cohn, who in his book on *The Writer's Way in France* has discussed the connection between the romantic situation in literature and the twentieth-century situation. He has mentioned what he calls the "problem of identity." This problem seems to me to center in a very complex development from romanticism to existentialism, then to what lies beyond the range of classic existentialism, as it is phrased in Kierkegaard, Sartre, Heidegger, and perhaps even Buber.

I suspect that Dubuffet and Beckett have broken through some of the boundaries of existentialist thought along new salients where existentialism itself is being revised by the artist. I have found no accepted name for this revision, but have called it a post-existentialist humanism. Some of these post-existentialist tendencies are referred to in books that appeared too late to be of much use to me—Martin Esslin's *Theatre of the Absurd*, and Richard N. Coe's *Ionesco*, which, I believe, supports my feeling that a residue of humanism persists, illogically enough, in our world where there is a "void at the center of things." As long as man is aware of this void and of the absurdity of his position in it, there is some locus for a sort of humanism, even if it be unlike any kind of humanism held in the past by cultures based upon a different world from ours.

This use of the term humanism is, I know, paradoxical; for how can there be a humanism when the self seems to be extinguished? Yet here is precisely the problem we meet in Beckett and Dubuffet, who find it impossible to escape from a consciousness of their own negligibility and of the nonsensicality of their world. The existentialists had already run into this problem, and there is no denying that Beckett and Dubuffet have the closest kinship with existentialism. But have they not in certain directions moved outside it? Their breakthrough seems to me to have an intimate connection with the breakthrough in science too; for I gather that the physicist or topologist has moved outside his own concepts just as the artist has moved outside his art. That is, science and art have found it necessary to displace man outside himself, all the while sensing what the cost of this displacement is. The humanism consists in the sense of this cost, a sense that we cannot ignore. If, then, the term humanism seems anomalous, the anomaly is due to the situation in which we find ourselves. Man cannot alienate himself from his own consciousness, a dilemma that brings on the present crisis in anti-literature and anti-art.

It is too soon to tell whether a-literature, anti-literature, anti-theater, anti-painting, and—so to speak—anti-science can really afford us foundations for a new humanism. But the question is there before us. I conjecture that Albert Camus may have a direct bearing on this question, and therefore at the close I return to him even if his work is done, and even if he did not write a-literature. It is not unthinkable that Camus, who lived very close to the heart of our modern darkness, may have been a little in advance of other artists and may already have heralded a reaction against anti-literature. This would be a surprising anachronism; yet I suggest it as a possibility.

In any case I am convinced that recent literature and painting must somehow be brought into relation with what is happening in modern thought, and that our interpretation will be better if we look back to the romanticisms of the nineteenth century to see how the romantic affirmation of the self was followed by a rejection of the self. I am aware that the nineteenth century was badly at odds with itself; however, by an oversimplification that may be allowed for the instant, I should like to isolate the theme that the romantic-liberal tradition created an idea of the self we have not only rejected but destroyed.

━━ ━━ ━━ ━━ ━━ ━━ ━━ ━━ ━━ ━━ ━━ ━━

ONE

The New Man as Functionary

I

We do not have to read contemporary literature to know that we are living in an age of togetherness, that Americans have accepted their own special kind of collectivism as it appears in the life of the organization man, whose existence is a mode of conforming to large enterprise. It would seem that individualism has been abandoned on both sides of the iron curtain; and I am surprised we have not paid more attention to Robert Musil, a novelist whose work has a title deeply symbolic of such an existence—*The Man Without Qualities* (*Der Mann ohne Eigenschaften*). The hero of this novel, Ulrich, is the man without qualities, and he realizes one day in 1913 as he strolls through Vienna that the events in his life have not really depended on himself, that something had its way with him, "like flypaper with a fly." He feels that he lives only with a sort of neutrality, that his experiences are not truly his own—or, rather, that experiences are now detachable from men, simply in the air, and that the account of his life belongs in some report on society. He feels like "a human something floating about in a universal culture-medium." His existence is negative because he has been completely available to others, to causes, to events and forces, as if he were a kind of liquid capital. He is extremely disposable. Probably we all know what Ulrich means to say when he notes that the center of gravity no longer lies in the individual but in the relations between things. So he decides there is a "magnificent inevitability" about our lives as a result of the division of labor—magnificent because it is the guise under which we feel the indifference of the forces that subject us to our own modern sort of fate. Our life is an involuntary repetition of certain activities, like the nest-building of birds, and our selves are constructed of standard materials according to a few efficient methods.

Ulrich is depressed by a sense that his existence has been manipulated: but by what? One of his friends calls him a man without qualities because such men appear by the millions nowadays: "It's the human type our time has produced." Through a hypersensitivity to his condition, Ulrich feels helpless and unfulfilled; his life seems to him like "an unwritten poem." He accounts for this disenchantment and frustration by saying that "mathematics has entered like a demon" into us until "we have gained in terms of reality, and lost in terms of the dream." He feels cheated, as if he were living by default, since his acts are all influenced by circumstances over which he has no control whatever. One of his friends has a name for this new fatality: the law of diminished responsibility. Ulrich doubts that his most private acts are his own: they belong in a great complex of events robbing them of any essence by which they might be called his.

He knows that he is capable of every virtue and every

vice; but his virtues and vices are alike negligible when their true meaning is entirely beyond the range of his own opinions, wishes, or judgments. He does not believe that he is victimized by circumstances; yet he does feel alienated from himself by these circumstances: "All moral events," he explains, "took place in a field of energy, the constellation of which charged them with meaning. . . . In this manner an endless system of relationships arose in which there was no longer any such thing as independent meanings, such as in ordinary life, at a first crude approach, are ascribed to actions and qualities. In this system the seemingly solid became a porous pretext for many other meanings." On account of the diffusion of responsibility, Ulrich feels everything faintly and with a weariness suggesting to him "what is always happening in Nature, namely that every play of forces tends in the course of time towards an average value and average condition, a compromise and a state of inertia." Ulrich is afflicted by a sense of living in a waste land. But he knows the reason better than Prufrock: he has only a surrogate existence, and "as a man within the man he lives not only in the scientist but in the businessman, in the administrator, in the sportsman, in the technician—even if for the present only during those main parts of the day that they call not their life but their profession."

Ulrich, it happens, is a mathematician—a mathematician who cannot cease being a man also; and Musil is saying much the same thing as C. P. Snow, whose novels so neatly state what happens to modern man when he takes part, as he must, in the organizations of power we now command. Snow's heroes are executive personalities dehumanized in a very special way since their real life is lived at the level of policy—policy made by intrigue within committees where each member is willing to manipulate others but where final decisions are detached from any individual responsibility. These new men are available and disposable; they are lonely and thwarted; they do not communicate partly because they cannot. Their true being is official—so official that their private selves are only a hindrance to the larger operation of the policies they formulate. They know, like Musil's character Arnheim, the industrialist, that today power must operate impersonally. They suffer from claustrophobia, since they are hemmed in and completely dominated by operations that fascinate them. Their anxiety rises not only from indecision about policy but also from inability to detach themselves, their residue of personal feeling, from the considerations on which they fiercely fix their attention. Their tactics in the committee room, their command over the inconceivable forces at their disposal, give them no sense of triumph, no assurance, no satisfaction because they also know they are powerless. Yet they have the appetite for power—what Snow calls "the intricate, labyrinthine and unassuageable rapacity, even in the best of men," for "men do not alter because the issues they decide are bigger scale." Even when they win, their victory is not theirs; for they too exist in a dominion of apparatus. And although, as Snow tells us, they have a clear vision of the future, they are aware they are moving as blindly into that future, and as inevitably, as the men whose future they are making. They work and argue under agonizing restraints, deprived of any capacity to love even while they are forced into intimate relations with others. Ulrich says to his sister, "It's so easy to have the energy to act and so difficult to find a meaning for action."

Long before Snow wrote of our new men, Musil suggested that such figures are not men but only functionaries, who can cause avalanches of suffering without being accountable in any private sense of the term. The problems have become too large-scale to be individual; and as Musil says, the real trouble is that the division of our activities is excellently organized but "we have neglected to create institutions to look after their correlation." Thus we have moved into a tragic arena of huge scope, where men of the highest intelligence make decisions that may be not only blind but vicious. It is not the tragic arena of nineteenth-century science with its iron laws remorselessly governing the universe; for there was a certain consolation, if not exhilaration, in the prospect of a cosmic determinism to which we are all subject. Before the trampling march of unconscious power—as Bertrand Russell put it—it was possible to take a certain defiant attitude that looked something like nobility.

The inevitability of the nineteenth-century scientific universe excluded any sense of guilt, any sense of responsibility, any malaise of conscience. Even Alfred North Whitehead was able to write as late as 1925 how the laws of physics have their own solemnity and are like decrees of fate. The functionaries in C. P. Snow's novels cannot be this stoic: they know they are answerable for purposes they have even against their will. They are agents of a destiny they themselves contrived, but which had to be contrived. So they are in a worse state than Hardy's Jude the Obscure, for they are without innocence and pathos, and they cannot assume that fate is bad luck, or a malign god, or the iron laws of nature. The functionary like Lewis Eliot must fit his conscience to majority policy, but he carries the burden of appraising that policy with his conscience. He suffers from a special sort of tragic dilemma, which involves a sense of acting in bad faith.

In other words we find ourselves in a position where man makes decisions that are effectual, but is no longer at the center of the universe where these decisions are made— since the decisions are not, in the older use of the word, his own. His determinations are not his, although he reached them. Musil notes that the anthropocentric attitude has been dissolving for centuries; the dissolution has now affected the personality itself, as we see in the alienated lives of Snow's new men, who have great force of will but nevertheless find themselves insignificant in the huge distances over which modern power operates. As Musil says, they press a white shining button, and what happens at the other end of the line is justified by a policy which cannot be called theirs although they wrought it.

It is perfectly clear, as Musil's hero sees, that we are continually destroying the moral self while we keep hoping that our old moral contrivances can hold our organizations together. This is the insecurity of deciding anything in an era of "advanced technique." Under the dominion of apparatus, the self acts, but acts do not express the self or lead to any assertion of the self or any sense of self-fulfillment. Jaspers has said all this is a result of our living in an artificial landscape of our own making, so that not science, but man in the realm of science, has entered a critical stage. To adapt the self to the new realities of power is to feel a new kind of dread, to sense a new kind of guilt, to be weighted by a new kind of helplessness quite different from our helplessness before either the gods or the natural order.

II

We have already reached the crux of our problem: Is it possible, while the individual is vanishing behind the functionary throughout the technological world, to have any sort of humanism that does not depend upon the older notions of the self, the independent self that is outdated or at least victimized by the operations of power on its present scale? Any such humanism must come to terms with our sense of the anonymity of the self, must therefore get beyond any romantic notion of selfhood. The importance of recent painting and literature is here, for both suggest that we must no longer confuse humanism with romantic individuality or with an anthropomorphic view that put the self at the center of things. I take the phrase from Jean Grenier's essay on the disappearance of man from art: "We now walk in a universe where there is no

echo of 'I.' " The image of the self held in past eras has been
effaced from the universe in which even nature seems to be
an abstraction.

Perhaps this does not mean that humanism is entirely
inaccessible. What we evidently need is a new impersonal
sense of the person, a retreat to a self that appears after the
assassination of the self occurring in an age dominated by
nuclear physics. It is clear that I am speaking in contradictions. Indeed, I am using what is called a logic of contradiction, a logic that accepts the illogicalities inherent in reality
in order to gain a new sort of immediacy in dealing with
the impasse in our existence. Or, as Musil has it, the old
contrivances of ethics and reason will not do. Any such
impersonal humanism will be tentative and defensive—may
even seem to be desperate; but it will be authentic as any
outworn idea of humanism cannot. It is a kind of humanism
emerging in writers and painters whose art is a conciliation
with *avant-garde* scientists, the scientists who have at last
seriously undertaken to exclude the anthropomorphic from
their speculations and to observe nature neutrally. Science
has always had an ideal of neutrality, but until recently did
not succeed in displacing the observer from the center of
the universe that is observed. We shall come to that, later.

We are concerned with literature, and our authentic contemporary literature is accurately called, by a logic of contradiction, anti-literature or a-literature, or a sabotage of
literature. Much of this literature has a new degree of
impersonality; the self is neutralized much as it is neutralized
in *avant-garde* science. It is the literature written by Samuel
Beckett, Nathalie Sarraute, and Eugène Ionesco; and it goes
along with the anti-painting done by Jean Dubuffet, Jean
Fautrier, and César Domela, all of them anti-artists corresponding to the anti-hero in the anti-novel or anti-drama.
These contradictions can be extended into science itself, for
there has recently appeared what might be called anti-
science, a science based upon concepts that are contradic-

tory, a science willing to accept inconsistency as a premise to any mathematical system we can devise. It is a science that has leaped beyond the old logic of cause and effect and has replaced certainties by probabilities. It has entertained concepts of anti-matter.

All this will remind us how Ortega y Gasset many years ago proposed that a "fundamental revision of man's attitude toward life is apt to find its first expression in artistic creation and scientific theory." If the artist is a good one, he may feel this revision of life even before the scientist. Then the rest of us catch up.

Back in 1947 Hugo von Hoffmansthal noted the importance of Bertolt Brecht's epic theater, which violated the laws of conventional drama before Ionesco did: "Our time is unredeemed," von Hoffmansthal said in his prefatory note to Brecht's *Baal:* "And do you know what it wants to be redeemed from? The individual. . . . We are anonymous . . . . Individuality is an arabesque we have discarded. I should go so far as to assert that all the ominous events we have been witnessing . . . are nothing but a very awkward and long-winded way of burying the concept of the European individual in the grave it has dug for itself."

Von Hoffmansthal was not alone, of course, in suspecting that we have grown weary of the burden of the self. During the forties it was fashionable to discuss our failure of nerve, and T. S. Eliot made his own tentative diagnosis of this malady in *The Cocktail Party*, treating the character of Edward Chamberlayne as a clinical case suffering from the conviction of his own insignificance. Edward tells the oracular Reilly that he has ceased to believe in his own personality; and Reilly assures Edward that this feeling is a serious and common affliction. It cannot be cured in a sanatorium; rather, it requires self-sacrifice, or dedication to a faith about which Reilly is carefully evasive. In fact, Reilly is an evangelist whose gospel seems important because it is not stated. But there is no doubt what is wrong with Edward, who shows all the symptoms of a man without qualities, and who is as weary as Ulrich.

Ortega y Gasset had an opinion that this fatigue set in at the height of the nineteenth century, the century of individualism, with its official liberal thought which was too closely allied with an economics of free enterprise and laissez faire. This century, which stressed the freedom of the rugged, anarchic self, also accepted a notion of utility, the greatest good for the greatest number, the theme of a collective welfare. Thus occurred a disastrous clash between the ideals of individual liberty and social well-being, a clash that in the long run irreparably damaged the whole liberal ideology of the nineteenth century. That is why Ortega remarks very wisely that the liberalism of the nineteenth century took inadequate precautions against collectivism; for by an irony in our Western culture the democratic ideals of freedom of the individual at last resolved themselves into a regime of collective mediocrity, as John Stuart Mill called it. Nietzsche was the one who saw the hypocrisy built into the liberal thought of his day: freedom for the self in a society of mass men. So Nietzsche preferred the self that was really free, the superman who owed the herd nothing but his contempt.

The sociologists say that individualism was only a transitional phase between two types of social organization, the *ancien régime* and the new collectivism. Kierkegaard himself at the heart of the nineteenth century noted that the "single one" is a category through which the self must pass during the course of a dialectic by which the self finds the self. In so saying, Kierkegaard defines the problem to which Martin Buber has devoted himself a century later: the question of the single one, which can be settled, as Buber sees it, only in a new dialectic between I and Thou, between Man and Man—a dialectic required constantly to prevent the self from being obliterated by the abstraction called Society. Buber has written that "The last generation's intoxication with freedom has been followed by the present generation's craze for bondage." The question of the single one, Buber fears, is answered today by "that powerful modern point of view, according to which in the last resort only so-called objectives, more precisely collectives, are real, while significance is attached to persons only as the workers or the tools of the collectives." The era of total individualism yields to the era of total groupism. And how can humanism survive in an age of total groupism? This is a crisis the humanist has not previously faced. No wonder the humanism that persists, if it does, in anti-literature and anti-painting persists only in residual form. No wonder it is hard to identify it as humanism at all. It is, at best, a salvage operation—indeed, the most desperate salvage operation ever attempted by the artist. Yet we must ask whether anti-literature has been able to salvage something quite as authentic, in its minimal way, as the confident romantic selfhood.

Before considering the new anonymous humanism, we must glance at the course by which the romantic idea of the self, deeply involved in the whole program of democracy and the whole performance in nineteenth-century arts, has exhausted itself in our hysteria to escape from the self by means of collectives.

The Romantic Self

I

Romanticism, which reached its peak in the nineteenth century, was a self-limiting disturbance. It created the self and destroyed the self. It created the self as a means of encountering the abuses of an *ancien régime*. As Camus said, the nineteenth century opened to the sound of falling ramparts. It destroyed the self because it held a notion of the self that was not tenable very long. Camus, who profoundly understood the meaning of romanticism, pointed out that the rebel, the archetypal romantic hero, finds himself in a precarious position. For one thing, he is constantly faced with the temptation to take part in revolutions, and revolutions always end by demanding conformism and thus always have to liquidate the rebels that inspired them. For another thing, the very act of resistance is essentially negative unless it leads the self beyond a mere posture of defiance.

In his classic analysis of the rebel Camus brings the romantic movement into focus by indicating the grandeur and the peril of rebellion, which is, to be sure, one of the essential dimensions of man, but which too often makes liberty synonymous with heroism. In short, romanticism is a form of irresponsible freedom.

The romantic rebels left to their followers, the liberals of the next generation, the difficult task of reaching a more responsible kind of individualism. And the liberals did not, understandably enough, succeed very well in solving this problem. The ideal of the romantic self proved, unfortunately, to be a very temporary category of individualism. Indeed, the romantics themselves often found the self to be an intolerable burden, and heroism often collapsed into tedium, ennui, if not despair or cynicism. Buber, too, has summarized the romantic dilemma in a sentence: "The word 'I' remains the shibboleth of mankind. Napoleon spoke it without power to enter into relation, but he spoke it as the *I* of a consummation. He who strives to say it as he said it only betrays the desperateness of his own self-contradiction."

Romanticism was, in effect, an artistic phase of the enlightenment that originated far back in the eighteenth century; it was essentially a counterattack of the self on the world outside—on the world invented by Descartes and Newton and the scientists who followed them. As everybody has noted, Descartes cleft apart the realm of man's experience: there was the *res extensa*—the realm of matter, operating by universal mathematical laws—and the *res cogitans*—the world inside, which by contrast with the actuality and regularity of the physical system outside, seemed unreal. The scientist who dealt with this physical system seemed to have a monopoly on truth; and the inward world, the world of feelings, impressions, sensibilities, appeared to be only an imperfect reflection of the world outside. As all

the psychologists of the eighteenth century said, the imagination is only a secondary activity.

We need not review the history of romanticism to show
how Schopenhauer spoke for all the romantics by reaffirming
the self against the *res extensa,* asserting that the world is
my idea of the world, a creation of my own will and idea.
By establishing its own world the romantic self rebelled
against the tyranny of a mechanical, impersonal world order.
Even more decisively, more naïvely, than Faust, Byron's
Manfred strikes the pose of defiant romantic heroism when
alone on the peak of the Jungfrau, isolated from men, from
the church, from nature, from divinity, he says "I was my
own destroyer and will be my own hereafter." This defiance,
this alienation of the willful self, is an early form of the
anarchy from which Nietzsche's free spirit suffered. At its
extreme, the romantic ideal of freedom is a form of *dis*-
relationship of the self from other selves. As the supreme
nihilist of his century, Nietzsche is the apostle of total
romantic freedom, which makes man an unconditioned and
creative will. Nietzsche is an arch individualist in an age of
individualism, projecting the notion of the self to minus
infinity.

These rebels equated freedom with heroism; and along
with Manfred there is the figure of Shelley's Prometheus,
the spirit of man liberated, who has created from the very
wreck of his hopes a vision of the self scepterless, free,
uncircumscribed—pinnacled in the intense inane. We know
that Shelley could not rest in this vision as final, for he,
unlike many romantics, yearned to enter into some sympathetic dialogue with his fellow men. This dialectic expresses itself in his theory of democracy, a dialectic that
runs through all his prose, his philosophic views of reform,
where he sees very clearly that freedom must be social as
well as personal. Setting aside his poetic and Promethean
vision of the self, he understands long before Marx wrote
his *Manifesto* that freedom cannot be gained by isolated

heroisms but only in the course of history in a struggle later known as the class war. "Morals and politics," he asserts, "can only be considered as portions of the same science." Although Shelley rejects violence as a revolutionary tactic, he knows that freedom is a social value based upon man's right to a return upon his own labor, upon his claim to a subsistence wage. More important, Shelley did not make the mistake most of the romantics made: that of identifying liberty with political rights alone; for when the romantics tried to conceive the self in action, in history, they too often were committed to a merely political program of extending the franchise. The only political program that concerned most romantics was a democratic ideal that had already been corrupted by a middle-class notion of laissez-faire economics.

Shelley's ideals of freedom are of extreme importance because they show how romanticism in literature and liberalism in political science were only two aspects of the same movement, which was indelibly middle class. The liberals, in fact, accepted many of the romantic notions of freedom, then added the notion of utilitarianism, the greatest good for the greatest number, even though this very utilitarian ideal was at odds with the firmly held notion of laissez-faire economics. It is evident that the liberal utilitarians were as sadly confused as the romantics were in literature. The premises of liberalism were romantic—the premises clustering about the freedom of the self—but the program of the liberals was utilitarian in practice, always stressing the welfare of society as a whole. The romantic vision of the self is the literary counterpart of the economic man who must take his risk alone in an open market; but both the romantic poets and the liberals talked a great deal about "the real interests of all." A poet like Shelley and a liberal like John Stuart Mill must be seen together if we are to get at the middle-class ideals of liberty permeating nineteenth-century thought.

As one who represents the best tradition of liberalism Mill comes face to face with the dilemma of reconciling the ideal of the free self with the need to bring this free self into relations with society. Mill was quite aware of the clash between what he called "rights" and what he called "duties," and he was honest and intelligent enough to realize that this clash between rights and duties was unresolved. In his essay *On Liberty* Mill is above all anxious to protect the rights of the individual against infringements by the state. Like all good liberals he hates *étatisme*, and tries to think of society as atomized into a number of individuals each endowed with liberty, especially with the economic liberty to truck, barter, and exchange in an unregulated "natural" market where self-interest can have the fullest play. On the other hand he knows well enough that free enterprise means collision, injury, and injustice. We have an obligation to society, which implies that our rights must somehow be restricted. Thus he phrases the problem in an insoluble way: Where is the limit at which my rights cease and yours begin; where is a boundary at which my liberty must be checked by my duty to others? Mill is never able to answer this question, for he realizes, as he says, that each part of a person's conduct is able to influence, directly or indirectly, the other persons with whom he exists in society. Whether I will or no, I affect "the others" even by what I do in my "private" as well as in my "public" life. Mill was often inclined to presume that one's rights are "private" and one's duties "public." This is a casuistry, and he was never happy with it. Inherent in Mill's scheme of rights was a figment that was taken as a premise of laissez-faire economics, the figment that if each one earnestly follows his own interests, somehow a general benefit results—a curious and rationalistic optimism. The only way Mill can deal with this collision between the rights of competing individuals is to urge that "private" rights be protected and that conscience be invoked to avoid injuring others. Especially must the rights of minorities be safeguarded against the weight of majorities. Yet the majority must have power to make decisions for the collective good. And Mill, of all liberals, saw the danger inherent in majorities—that they not only tend to dominate minorities but also drift toward being mere collective mediocrities.

Very ill at ease with his liberalism, Mill was one of the first to recognize what was involved when the free self, an essentially romantic image, entered into relations with society. He suspected that the ideal of liberty, on which romantic liberalism was based, was incompatible with the greatest good for the greatest number, the collective principle on which Bentham and the utilitarians founded their liberal democracy. In a word, Mill saw what Ulrich saw a good deal later—that individual liberty is negated by the laws of sociology.

The fifth chapter of Mill's autobiography is called "A Crisis in My Mental History." Actually, it is a crisis in romantic-liberal thought, and a point at which an originally romantic idea of the self begins to change over into an existential idea of selfhood—the self as being "engaged" with "others." During the winter of 1826-1827, while the brightness of Shelley's romantic vision was still in the air, Mill, who had been reared to believe in the most enlightened Benthamite notions, suddenly made the melancholy discovery that the whole liberal program for bettering society had nothing whatever to do with the happiness of the individual: in the midst of social progress he was deeply troubled to feel that his own existence had dried up, that he was weary, cheated, and unfulfilled. Here he was in the afterglow of the romantic movement feeling exactly what Ulrich felt a century later. The entire liberal system all at once seemed to have no relevance to his own inward life, and thus lost its "charm" for him. He was forced to ask himself a pitiless question: "Suppose that all your objects in life were realized; that all the changes in institutions

24

and opinions which you are looking forward to, could be completely effected at this very instant: would this be a great joy and happiness to you?" Sadly he felt compelled to answer No. He seemed to have nothing personal left to live for; his life no longer seemed to be really his, but only a derivation of the institutions that molded it. He felt, in brief, like a hollow man, one whose spirit is impoverished, one whose self is merely a byproduct of social laws. This is a remarkable and revealing experience to have occurred during the romantic-liberal period. Mill describes his sense of frustration, his alienation from himself, much as Ulrich does; he calls it a conflict between free will and fatalism, or "Philosophical Necessity." The existentialists would say that Mill's life lacked authenticity.

Even the attendant symptoms are Ulrich's symptoms. Mill had, he says, a depressing sense that all his pleasures, his passions, his virtues were undermined. He saw that he had been working toward ends for which he had no real desire, for they would make him a man without qualities. In despair he tried to stimulate his feelings, to quicken his benumbed sensitivities, by reading Marmontel and Wordsworth, hoping that these romantic writers would support the "internal culture of the individual." By exciting his sentiments he hoped to counteract the barren externality of a life devoted to bringing about material improvements in society. It is evident that as early as 1826 Mill was already aware of Martin Buber's problem—how to resist the impersonal and institutional nature of our activity by finding some axis within the self. In *I and Thou* Buber writes: "Institutions are 'outside,' where all sorts of aims are pursued, where a man works, negotiates, bears influence, undertakes, concurs, organizes, conducts business, officiates, preaches . . . . Feelings are 'within,' where life is lived and man recovers from institutions."

Mill identified the problem, but he never solved it. He was not able to find this existential axis, perhaps because he was too much a liberal ever to give up his faith in institutions. In spite of his depression, in spite of his effort to cultivate his feelings, he remained, he says, "as much as ever a Radical and Democrat." He adds: "I often said to myself, what a relief it would be if I could disbelieve the doctrine of the formation of character by circumstances." But unlike the coarser, less sensitive liberals of his age, he suffered personally from the desiccating effects of liberalism on the person, the minimizing of the self by the law of large numbers.

The malady was endemic in the nineteenth century, and Ortega y Gasset is quite accurate in his diagnosis: the older liberalism did not sufficiently safeguard the person against collectivism. The liberals who romantically believed in freedom staked their faith in systems. As a result, the romantic belief in liberty proved to be incompatible with the liberal belief in programs for the progress of society. The nineteenth-century liberals were devoted to both individualism and institutions; they had faith in both freedom and necessity, and never satisfactorily adjusted the two. They inherited from the romantics the conviction that freedom is a good in itself. The romantics never asked whether freedom is good for the individual; and the liberals, as Ortega says, were convinced that freedom is good for society. To bring freedom to society, they relied upon institutions; so romantic individualism became liberal collectivism. The liberal program for society finally negated the significance of the person. Freedom became an organization, and a middle-class organization at that.

Once again Musil's novel shows—even more decisively than Mill's autobiography—what happened to individualism after liberalism resolved itself into an institutional program for progress, a constantly more extensive statistical calculation. Ulrich meditates how for us the individual life is not so real as the actuarial laws by which we get at the meaning of the individual life: "For instance, the statistics of divorce in America. Or the proportion between the male and female birth-rates, which is, of course, one of the most constant ratios. And then you know that every year there is a fairly constant number of conscripts that try to escape military service by means of self-mutilation. Or that every year approximately the same percentage of the population of Europe commits suicide." These large numbers are constants; the persons involved are variables. And we depend, if we can, on the constants. C. P. Snow tells us how the question of saturation bombing of civilians was decided, rightly or wrongly, according to such calculations. Mill called this impersonal view of things philosophical necessity. It is sardonic that a liberalism sprung from the ideal of a free self should end by granting the self only a statistical existence.

That is, the abstraction is more valid than the items on which the abstraction is based; so, as Ulrich remarks, our lives lose meaning except in a statistical context: "One person commits suicide for this reason, and another for that reason, but when you have a very large number, the accidental and personal element ceases to be of interest, and what is left is—well, what *is* left?" The average. But nobody has the slightest idea what the average really is, for behind the laws of collectivity there is an assumption that the particular instance does not matter much: "And the highest meaning turns out to be something that can be got at by taking the average of what is most profoundly senseless." Thus, as Ulrich explains, we empty out the meaning of our lives, which signify something only when they fit into a graph. "And if it were not for this law of averages, nothing might happen in one year, and there would be no certainty about anything for the next year." The laws by which we now live seem to Ulrich like the kinetic theory of gases: "Everything swirls about chaotically, each thing doing what it likes, but if one calculates what in a manner of speaking has no cause to arise out of it, one finds that it is the very thing that does really arise!" The only real value is the average, and Ulrich wryly concludes that our personal motion—to right or to left, this way or that—"is of no consequence to the average value."

Ulrich is recapitulating how romantic individualism was perverted into a collectivism dominated by the law of large numbers, bringing with it a sense of diminished responsibility. Alfred North Whitehead once underscored the dilemma by saying that the radical inconsistency in modern thought is our firm belief in man as a self-determining organism and our equally firm belief in the validity of deterministic laws.

By retrospect we see that there is a nearly tragic irony in this negating of the romantic self by the very liberalism born of the romantic ideal—a dramatic reversal from freedom to necessity. The heroic figure of free man—a dream of the enlightenment, the Promethean self pinnacled in the steady bright light of the eternal, beyond time and history—is plunged into the institutional lower world where the law of large numbers closes in and the average is a prison where the self loses identity. Prometheus is bound again, cast into a utilitarian order where his freedom is gone and his existence is only a form of contingency, depending upon numerical constants. Thus appears the existential theme of *Geworfenheit*—the state of being "thrown" into a world where we do not "belong." It is a second exile of man, doubly melodramatic because the romantic vision of the free self is so intense.

II

In spite of the disaster that befell the romantic self, the deeper drama of the nineteenth century was still to be played: the existential drama. For the romantic problem of freedom led directly into the more searching and private problem of authenticity—in what sense we have an existence that is really "ours." This existential problem inevitably arose from the romantic-liberal dilemmas. After the romantic self was neutralized by the pressure of collectives, the question of authenticity remained, for we have an existence even after we have lost our singularity. The romantic quest for freedom changed into the existential quest for an authentic self capable of being identified and sustained amid the average. If the romantic rebellion was against God and kings, the existential rebellion was at first against "the others." An existential self must be earned against a banal majority. However, the first generation of existentialists were deeply affected by romantic heroism, so that Kierkegaard and Nietzsche, for example, maintained their authenticity against the others with a defiance that was a sign of their desperation. Like Manfred, they were immoralists.

Existentialism entered its critical phase when it had to qualify this romanticism, and when Kierkegaard's "question of the single one" yielded gradually, perhaps under the influence of liberals like Mill, to Buber's dialectic between man and man. The existentialist dilemmas were inherent in romanticism, for sooner or later Prometheus had to come face to face with the philistines—and Buber, more successfully than Kierkegaard or Nietzsche, has reached a coexistence with the collective mediocrity. Romantic freedom was an absolute; existential freedom is a contingency, not a right. The self could no longer live at a romantic height of Being (*Sein*) but eventually found its more authentic existence at the humbler level of *Dasein*, of a man in his particular and personal situation, existing not absolutely but only contingently, moment by moment, in time, here and now, when each instant is a crisis. This existence forces us to come to terms with what is local, with history, and compels us to negotiate with the commonplace and conventional as Shelley's Prometheus never had to. The main post-romantic task is to identify the irreducible minimum of our experience that can be honestly identified as our own. Thus the question of our identity is the question of our authenticity; and the question of authenticity involves also the question to what extent we are "engaged" with others. If the romantic freedom was a mode of alienation from society, the existential freedom is a way of maintaining one's integrity in society.

In sum, the nineteenth century posed existential questions much more urgent than the rather naïve romantic questions, and as we look back over the romantic and post-romantic era we see how compelling the need for authenticity was: more compelling than the need for "freedom." Goethe's Faust was a romantic hero who faced an existential crisis when he plunged into existence and found that he could not seduce Gretchen without having to pay the penalties that Manfred and Don Juan, "free" as they were, never had to pay. But it is Carlyle's hero Diogenes Teufelsdroeckh who shows during the course of *Sartor Resartus* how the romantic crisis changed into the existential crisis barely a generation after Byron had set Manfred alone on the Jungfrau making defiant gestures. Teufelsdroeckh finds that his romantic free will is "hemmed in" by duties to those who exist with him, contingently, in time, in a society where the self must be "annihilated": "For man lives in Time, has his whole earthly being, endeavour and destiny shaped for him by Time: only in the transitory Time-Symbol is the ever-motionless Eternity we stand on made manifest."

Teufelsdroeckh is tormented by an existential problem that an earlier hero like Manfred could ignore—the problem of I and Thou. Accordingly he is driven by a compulsion to do his duty, to feel that he must commit himself to others; and he finds, like Mill, that a simple laissez-faire assertion of rights does not suffice. Teufelsdroeckh learns to "close his Byron and open his Goethe" and to "embrace man by pity." The lesson being learned by Carlyle's hero is still being taught by Martin Buber, who says that the romantic *I* was discordant with everything; but the existential *I* must stand in a personal relation with other selves and with the necessity called *It*. One way to resist the tyranny of the world of *It* is to subjugate the *It* to relations made between the *I* and "the others," creating an I-Thou relationship. Without this personal relation, the *I* is only an abstraction.

The existential barrier is closing in on Teufelsdroeckh, who finds that his "grim fire-eyed defiance" in the face of a dead mechanical universe is not enough; he accepts a new "worship of sorrow" when he strives to make his insurgent romantic self come to terms with time and society. His post-romantic *Weltschmerz* is a half-tragic recognition that "Our life is compassed round with Necessity; yet is the meaning of Life itself no other than Freedom, than voluntary Force: thus have we a warfare." This warfare ceases only when Teufelsdroeckh feels the "organic filaments" binding him to others in a world of relation. Nietzsche is driven mad by this anguish as he tries—in vain—to break through the existential barrier and recover the absolute liberty of the first romantic self, a free spirit, a Dionysiac reveler who ecstatically denies all repressions. It is a mistake to suppose that Nietzsche's commitment is to power; it is not power but freedom, joy, total liberation of the self of which Nietzsche dreams. Yet he too is wounded by his pity.

The disaster that overtook the romantic self in a democratic society was a tragic action in which the existential self transcended calamity by finding something more authentic than the romantics and liberals could offer with their notions of liberty and material happiness. This existential self—the self that feels above all a need for integrity—is born the moment so violent a thinker as Carlyle asks his most important question: "Who am I? The being who calls himself I?" Hamlet had asked this question at the threshold of the age of individualism. It was a query that nagged Stendhal, too, as he lay awake nights reflecting that he knew himself least of all, that he was a stranger to himself. Stendhal's heroes, like Hamlet, were always doubting who they really were. Julien Sorel tried to find his genuine self, the ground for being "sincere," by playing role after role, none of them suiting very long. If romanticism was a way of affirming the self by playing striking roles, enacting heroic gestures, the very gestures and roles provoked another demanding question: which role is the authentic one? Julien found, along with Hamlet, that the self may be an illusion, that we have no self but only selves with changing profiles as we act out our existence.

At moments we may be so carried away by the drama we are playing that the self seems to be not only convincing but enduring. Byron's Manfred was thus carried away, fixated upon the alluring image of his wicked past; he was arrested narcissistically at a moment when he had struck a diabolic posture, which was an excuse to escape from the present, from time, into an abstraction that enabled him to be what he willed to be. Of course the illusion could not last; there was always a crashing return to the present, showing the self to be different from the envisioned self, and unable to cope with the burden of the ordinary. The romantic vision of the self was often an evasion of the self, and long before Prufrock, Stendhal's characters unhappily suspected they were leading a sham existence, constantly preparing faces to meet the faces that they met.

It was another of the ironies of romanticism, which put the self at the center of reality, that the romantics tried to identify the self by means of passion, by will, by the decisive act, all the while there was only a rational fiction, or a dream, behind their assertion of the self. Byron and Shelley and Carlyle were all irrationalists in their own ways, and they should have known that the self can be reduced to a series of emotional states having little in common; yet by a kind of romantic rationalism they gave the self an identity, assuming it was constantly "there" somewhere behind conflicting moods and feelings. A few of the romantics avoided this rationalism: Wordsworth, for instance, who was always baffled by a "strangeness in the mind"—"A feeling that I was not for that hour/ Nor for that place." His sense of living in "unknown modes of being" is almost shamanistic, and explains why Wordsworth was more occupied with the authenticity of his experience, with the validity of what was "felt in the blood, and felt along the heart," than with abstract problems of freedom, rights, and political ideologies that attracted romantics like Shelley. It also explains why Wordsworth, devoted as he was to studying his feelings, was more deeply immersed in the mystery of time than romantics who tried to escape from time or deny time by holding a revolutionary vision of the future. On the whole the romantics intent upon their feelings were more conscious of the duplicity of the self than were those obsessed by the idea of liberty.

None of the writers of the nineteenth century was more mindful of the problem of authenticity than Matthew Arnold, whose work looks backward upon the two great themes we have been following: the romantic affirmation of the self and the liberal affirmation of the self, both of which seemed to him unsound. Throughout his verse and prose Arnold is drawn toward an ideal of authenticity as a substitute for romantic-liberal notions. In his melancholy verse Arnold writes as a post-romantic who has lost confidence in the passionate rebellious self "standing for some false impossible shore." Instead, he seeks some "knowledge of our buried life" flowing deep within, unregarded, and intuited only by vague echoes rising to consciousness from a hidden self so inaccessible it is like an "infinitely distant land." In his essays Arnold is always urging upon us a distinction between a "better" self and the "ordinary" self; he rejects the liberal theme of "doing as one likes," which he calls a mark of anarchy, and he insists that culture is being something, not having something. It is an "internal condition." Thus Arnold takes up again, and modulates, all the problems of the self that met the romantics and liberals. For him the romantic roles are empty, though the malaise lingers:

Hast thou then still the old unquiet breast,
Which neither deadens into rest,
Nor ever feels the fiery glow
That whirls the spirit from itself away,
But fluctuates to and fro,
Never by passion quite possessed
And never quite benumbed by the world's sway?
("A *Summer Night*")

Is there, he asks, no life but these: madman or slave, rebel
or conformist?

He is saddened by his visit to the Carthusian monastery
in the Alps, where he feels strongly the inauthenticity of
British civilization:

. . . We admire with awe
The exulting thunder of your race;
You give the universe your law,
You triumph over time and space!
Your pride of life, your tireless powers,
We laud them, but they are not ours.
("*Stanzas from the Grande
Chartreuse*")

Arnold sees, too, that the liberal self is a mask for the vulgar
man, *l'homme sensuel moyen,* or for the philistine whose
ideas are all mechanical. More despairingly than Mill he
was convinced that democratic freedom was only an abstraction, for the self and for society. It meant freedom for
a single class, and the class chose to be mediocre. The self,
having been invented as a category of rebellious heroism,
was absorbed into a collectivity so oppressive that democracy, a political cognate of romanticism, was in effect a
regime of ordinary people with stock notions. The self,
having been discovered by the romantics, was then devalued.

Arnold is saying what Ortega y Gasset has recently argued,
that within the context of the majority, the romantic-liberal

individual declined toward the mass man, and the technician became a culture-hero during the nineteenth century. Ortega says that the two inventions of this age were liberal democracy and technism; and the technical man is a prototype of the mass man, built hurriedly from a few stereotyped designs. Technical man—the forerunner of the modern self who is a functionary—is rooted in his specialism; he considers any wider culture dilettantism, and he "proclaims it as a virtue that he takes no cognizance of what lies outside the narrow territory specially cultivated by himself." So Ortega agrees with Arnold that the ordinary democratic man is without culture; for culture means criticism, and criticism is only the capacity for dissatisfaction and self-scrutiny. Without this capacity the ordinary man cannot have authenticity; he remains a creature limited by his self-satisfaction—what Arnold calls his provincialism—and his smugness is the more threatening because he has strong and vulgar appetites and the means for satisfying those appetites. Consequently his pseudo-existence is a mechanism for obliterating the self by cultivating inferior pleasures. It is significant that both Arnold and Ortega are apprehensive about the democratic commitment to fun. This commitment is not the less questionable when, as Dwight Macdonald has recently said, it takes a middlebrow air of culture. The indictment is the same, though the phrasing differs: Mill called this inauthenticity collective mediocrity; Arnold calls it *Gemeinheit*, commonness, or faith in machinery; Ortega calls it the vertical invasion of barbarians. The only hope of these critics was in the minority, the saving remnant, or those who are capable of "holding fast the hard doctrine of the unsoundness of the majority."

Meanwhile, along with this consolidation of the majority there came a new anxiety, for if one is to conform, then one must be assured he is normal. Thus the need for freedom is replaced by a need for therapy.

III

The decline and fall of the romantic self can be followed through its whole dismal course in the greatest nineteenth-century novel of the inauthentic—Flaubert's *Sentimental Education* (1869), in which Frédéric Moreau appears as the first modern man without qualities, the hero who retreats from all romantically held positions, who makes the first great refusal. He is an anti-hero. He shows what happened when the romantic hero capitulated to the middle class; or perhaps it would be better to say that the middle class absorbed and finally destroyed the romantic hero who at first symbolized this class. Frédéric is a hero who cannot sustain his roles.

The need to play roles was felt even in the romanticism of the eighteenth century, for Robert Lovelace, seducer of Clarissa Harlowe, is one of the earliest dandies, a type of culture-hero invented by the middle class. The figure of the dandy, on which Baudelaire fixed his attention, is one of the most ambiguous in romantic and post-romantic litera-ture. He is first of all a consequence of the fall of an *ancien régime* before a middle class—a substitute for the aristocrat who had lost caste. The dandy is a middle-class aristocrat, a figure who could make his entrance only in the cities that were becoming the milieu for the bourgeoisie. As Baudelaire put it: "A great tradition has been lost, and a new one is not yet established." The old "robust and martial form of life, a state of readiness on the part of each individual, which gave him a habit of gravity and of violence in his movements" lent the bygone aristocratic hero his stature. But the dandy appeared as an urban hero floating and drifting above "the underworld of our great city," the Paris of a new middle class. His life is a role.

Often the dandy wears the mask of the bohemian. Yet he is not really bohemian. He has a taste for the heroic, but there is no theater in which he can enact his heroisms. He must get along without the advantage of the "parade" furnished by a court. So he must resort to the studio, leading an artificial existence "before a mirror." The pageant of fashionable life is substituted for the regal parade, and the term "living in style" has a new meaning. Though the dandy is born of the middle class, he must devote himself to the trivialities, the expenditures, the affectations which belie the thrift, the caution, the seriousness of the middle class. The dandy cultivates a sensibility that came with the quasi-romanticism of the eighteenth century. He refines this sensibility to a fashionable heroism, which is a diluted insolence. The dandy is a pseudo-bohemian living in style. His feelings all cluster about his vanity as he watches and applauds himself; and his existence is a new sort of morality play devoted to the theme of pleasure—the diversions of an urban society as yet lacking any deep cultural or moral roots.

In what sense can the dandy live authentically? Like the romantic hero, he is in revolt against his society, its dullness and decency. Often his revolt takes the form of cultivating illusions—illusions about the figure of himself he must create. He makes his world from the ideas associated with his pose. Yet he can hardly have faith in these ideas, for he is intelligent enough to know that his existence is an artifice. Thus the dandy is a hero who has within the core of his existence an anti-heroic principle. He is hero and anti-hero at once. His most flagrant and fashionable gestures are open to ridicule. He is a rebel who disdains the mediocrity he sees about him; he must define his rather negative existence by being what others are *not*. "What have I to do in the world?" Frédéric Moreau asks his mistress. "Others struggle after riches, fame, power; I have no occupation." Frédéric says that his dream of Mme. Arnoux is the center of his life. It is hard to ground an identity for the self on this sort of exclusion, on this sort of dream. That is why a death of the heart is inherent in the existence of a dandy, who is always in danger of toppling into cynicism.

Instead of living authentically, he gives himself over to pleasure, for he has at his disposal the dominion of apparatus, as C. P. Snow calls it—the gadgets, conveniences, and utilities that have been furnished by the middle class. As a result the dandy's life becomes a sort of substitute for existence: he must live on the surface, at the exterior, amid the accessories which become his necessities. Above all, he must have illusions; and these give his figure a certain desperation, for he shows how we must have illusions after all illusions are lost, after there is no longer any chance to have illusions. The dandy suffers from a split in feeling that runs like a theme from the eighteenth century through the hesitations of J. Alfred Prufrock. Shelley's Prometheus, the defiant spirit of man, was heroic because he could hope until hope created from its own wrecks what it willed to contemplate. But the dandy yielded to the temptation to indulge himself instead of transcending himself. He marks the crackup of romantic idealism. The dandy is a realist; and Gautier speaks like a dandy when he says that for him the world exists. Perhaps this assurance that the world exists is one result of the city, which closed in, dismally, upon the dandy until he found it impossible to escape as the pastoral romantics did.

It is customary to call Flaubert a realist; but it would perhaps be better to consider his character of Frédéric Moreau as a minor romantic who lives in dreams, who reduces romanticism to sentimentality again, as it was in the eighteenth century. Frédéric spends his life charmed by his vision of Mme. Arnoux; but he is never able to love her, and his romantic passion dilutes itself to philandering as he watches his mistress grow old and his feelings for her dissolve into an illusion of experience. As he says to his friend Deslauriers, "Perhaps we let ourselves drift from our course." While he gluts his fancy with daydreams of loving

Mme. Arnoux, he gives himself to Rosanette, a creature of the flesh; to Louise Roque, the ugly heiress; to Mme. Dambreuse, the wealthy widow he cannot bring himself to wed. Flaubert called his novel a *Sentimental Education*. He might have used the title *Lost Illusions*. The illusions are lost because Frédéric, who tries to live by making one romantic gesture after another, really only wants security. He knows that the world exists, and he is content to let it overwhelm him. He hardly asks himself Prufrock's question: Do I dare? He does not dare, and thus becomes the anti-hero, the anti-romantic who says to himself "It was a time for realism." Refusing to take the risk, he sees his life run down into the sand. When Mme. Arnoux leaves him for the last time, he cannot bring himself to embrace her, for he fears that a disgust might follow; so he prudently rolls a cigarette. Then she steps into her carriage, which is soon lost to sight: "And that was all."

Because it is a novel of disenchantment, it is called realistic; but ironically Frédéric loses contact with reality at the heart of his realism. He proves how necessary were even the poor illusions of the dandy. Elizabeth Bowen has her own comment on this irony: "Illusions are art, and it is by art that we live, if we do." Frédéric failed even as dandy. Having avoided the romantic risks Julien Sorel was willing to take, Frédéric finds that he has solved nothing by his realism. "The atrophy of his heart had left his head entirely clear"—but at last he is stripped of even his dreams. His surrender to middle-class security leads him back to a waste land from which he had tried to escape by self-indulgence. Frédéric has lost the romantic self. He is a dandy who could not protect his studio values.

His illusions, in fact, were his disaster, as his dream of Mme. Arnoux proves. The first time he sees her on the Seine steamer is like the moment when Dante, wandering along the Lung' Arno sees Beatrice: it changes his life. "It was like a vision." There she was, seated on a bench in dazzling sunlight, her oval face, her dark skin, her work-basket striking Frédéric with amazement, as if she were an object from another world. "What was her name, her home, her life, her past?" Her image rouses in Frédéric a deep yearning, a limitless poignant curiosity. From that instant a romantic fantasy possesses him. The difficulty is to keep this illusion when Mme. Arnoux appears in her middle-class setting: when he visits her at Creil, in her husband's factory, and they wander through the rows of pottery, Frédéric is bored. In a panic he flees to the arms of Rosanette, where he is not vexed by any need for illusion.

Mme. Arnoux is a particular kind of fatal woman much like Emma Bovary—the fatal woman of the middle class, doubly fatal since she is commonplace, and can stimulate fantasies seriously damaging because they are in continual peril of colliding with actualities. The risk of disenchantment is immediate. This is a difference between Mme. Arnoux and Dante's Beatrice, or between Mme. Arnoux and Shelley's veiled maids, who never can be violated by life. Shelley can hold his vision intact even while he is disenchanted with the women he meets and loves; the women suffer, but the fantasy remains untarnished. The romantic vision keeps its enchantment by a distance that cannot be profaned. But Frédéric must nourish his day-dreams while he is visiting the Arnoux household in the rue Paradis-Poissonnière; there he finds a middle-class wife in a dressing gown caring for her son, who is crying and scratching his head: "Frédéric had been anticipating paroxysms of joy; but passionate feelings seldom survive a change of atmosphere, and, meeting Mme. Arnoux again in an unfamiliar setting, he felt that her stature was somehow diminished, that she had suffered an indefinable deterioration—in short, that she had changed."

The dandy's task was unheroic, but taxing nonetheless—to feed his illusions amid these deteriorations. His jeopardy was to be too keenly aware of the difference between the rue Paradis-Poissonnière and the mirror that gave back reassuringly the images of a glassy theater where he could play the roles he yearned to play. The dandy was forced to exploit the inauthenticity of his existence. He had not yet emptied the romantic self, but he could hardly avoid feeling a deepening cavity inside him.

The dandy is attended by his own pathos: he has a sense that society is fraudulent, but he also has a sense that his life is an imposture. His adventures never make him a hero; yet he thirsts for heroism in an age that is mediocre. Ortega said that the hero's life is a "perpetual resistance" to what is customary; and though Matthew Arnold did not call for heroism, he told the Victorians that they habitually lived in their ordinary selves. The dandy resists the ordinary, which is the inauthentic, but he fails to gain the authentic. He is an existential hero *manqué*.

Often he is driven to the confession as a means of easing his sense of inauthenticity. The romantics were often exhibitionists; they invested heavily in their personalities. But their self-revelations, their display of pain or sadness, were not in the confessional mood of the dandy, who is insecure, self-conscious, and finical. Baudelaire has this confessional note, even in his criticism. The figure of Frédéric Moreau resembles the figure of J. Alfred Prufrock, whose love song is a confessional. Prufrock is a belated dandy, speaking nervously, and in a plaintive vein, of his inauthentic selves. Like Frédéric, he must guard his illusions when, in the lamplight, bare and braceleted arms are downed with hair. Can he hear the mermaids sing? Dare he start a scene or two?

What began as a romantic assertion of the self—of a free, willful, often isolated self—changed into a mistrust of the self, a need for communion, adjustment, or therapy. The insolent and elastic Don Juan, a dandy who was able to take on epic stature, gives way to the melancholy half-bohemian Frédéric Moreau, whose authenticity evaporates into daydreams, whose existence is a course of alienation from himself, a way of capitulating to a class that has few illusions except its self-deceptions.

THREE

The Romantic Touch in Painting

I

The painter in the romantic era did not have to think out the question of freedom; he did not need any theories about who he was. In his revolt against bureaucratic, official, academic art he came to terms with the reality he represented by means of his touch—personally and at once. That is, he resolved the problem of authenticity almost before it was posed. From the very nature of his medium the romantic painter had an authenticity the romantic writers had to earn. For if romantic painting is anything, it is, with all its extremely different techniques and visions, a very direct counterattack of the self upon the world, a repudiation of academic formulas that stood between the painter and his own impression of things. To be sure, the romantic painter, like the romantic poet, often used the formulas of academic art, and romantic painting is filled with passages that are conventional or else unsuccessful attempts to render a personal vision. Nevertheless Delacroix, the arch romantic, spoke for all truly romantic painters when he said, "Mediocre painters never have sufficient daring; they never get beyond themselves. Method cannot supply a rule for everything; it can only lead everyone to a certain point." And Baudelaire, the one who best understood romantic painting, claimed that romantic art exists in an atmosphere created by the highly personal vision of the painter. Even more imperiously than the romantic poet, the romantic painter imposed himself on his world.

Method alone will not do: at this point the romantic painters parted company with academic painters. At the heart of the romantic impulse in painting was the desire to transcend a method or a medium, to use the old formulas personally, to make one's own experiment. This urge to transcend medium and method inevitably means that the romantic painter cannot be content with what is stated; he strives for what cannot be stated. There is a struggle to make the medium convey what the painter wishes it to convey. The course of nineteenth-century painting is marked by the effort to subject the painter's method to his sensibility. That is why Delacroix leads to Van Gogh and to Cézanne, who made agonizing attempts to "realize" his *petites sensations*. A romantic attitude runs through the whole century, giving the work of each major painter a high degree of authenticity.

Baudelaire, seeking this unison of expression, this genuine atmosphere, turned to Delacroix as the great romantic. In 1824 Delacroix wrote in his journal, "The things that are most real to me are the illusions which I create with my painting. Everything else is quicksand." He was driven by a need to express these illusions, which constantly drew him toward distant horizons—horizons beyond which Baudelaire glimpsed what was *new*: "All my days," says Delacroix, "lead to the same conclusion, an infinite longing for something which I can never have, a void which I cannot fill, an intense desire to create by every means." Like Keats, he saw everything as if he stood at charmed magic casements. Each of the great romantic painters, like Goya or Géricault, exploited as far as he could his private angle of vision, daring to create a world from his own idea of the world. As Delacroix said, "The material process which we call painting is no more than the pretext, the bridge between the mind of the artist and that of the beholder." Wordsworth said something very similar: he wanted the poet to carry his passion alive into the reader's heart as an immediate excitement. Perhaps few romantic poets have the immediacy of a painter like Delacroix, for whom painting was a language "capable of concentrating the effect of a moment." The enchantment in romantic painting is due to a harmony of mood that can instantaneously be felt, making the painter, as Delacroix remarks, "far more master of what he wants to express than the poet or musician." It is the harmony of a temperament, through which the world is refracted. Critics have spoken of the "imperialism" of romantic painting, by which they mean this subjecting the world to a temperament. Such imperialism asserts its authority not by method but rather by subduing things to the painter's eye.

Because of this intense effort to adapt the world to the eye, to transcend a medium or technique, there is no great difference between so-called romantic painting and so-called realistic painting; for the great realists strained their medium as relentlessly as the great romantics. What happened when a so-called realist like Daumier tried to present the horrors of revolution in his lithograph *Rue Transnonain?* Exactly what happened when Goya a few years earlier tried to represent the horrors of Napoleonic wars: out of what is essentially a cartoon, a caricature, a journalist's calligraphy arises a distortion as powerful as Rembrandt's— an art where the stark bodies of the slain are a shocking symbol of the absurd. This so-called realism is like the expressionist art of Van Gogh; for expressionism only extends this grotesquerie, and there is a deep note of the grotesque in Van Gogh's vision of his garden at Saint Rémy, seen through the eyes of someone trying desperately to speak his madness. Daumier's visions of Don Quixote are like the "enormous magic" of Baudelaire's vision. In fact Daumier more completely transcended his medium than Delacroix did; his imperialism was even more tyrannical.

Like the romantic poet, the romantic painter was reacting against the separation Descartes had made, back in the seventeenth century, between the world outside and the world inside, the *res extensa* and the *res cogitans*. Romantic painting is an *anti*-Copernican revolution in the arts by which man again stands at the center of the world he represents. The romantic painter even more intimately than the romantic poet made the world his personal construction.

This counterattack on the world is as evident in impressionism as it was in romanticism, for impressionism is really a very private and momentary view of nature. Take, for example, any of Monet's paintings of the Seine. None of us actually sees the river like this. Monet brings the scene into intimate—even fragile—touch with consciousness, by means of the eye, of course; and these landscapes are as truly an illusion as Delacroix's vision of the *Death of Sardanapalus*. Monet exploits his own sensations, and we must not be deceived by the talk about his broken palette, his analysis of light and color, his scientism.

Without doubt impressionism is not the same as romanticism; yet throughout the whole nineteenth century the painter was always trying to find out what the relation was between his consciousness and what was outside his consciousness. The significant meaning of romanticism in painting is that the temperament of the artist was directly involved with the world, giving his work a personal tonality or structure. Romantic painting re-introduced private values into artistic representation. It destroyed the false classicism that was only an academism—the notion that painting must be impersonal, traditional, and answerable to literary themes. When the artist's self became commanding, modern painting began.

In short, the romantic painter became conscious of the fact that he was conscious—even if it was a consciousness of things beyond himself. We can see this rather private occupation of the world starting about 1750 in the so-called realism of Chardin, who is unlike the Dutch realists of the seventeenth century, the century of Descartes. The Dutch realists treated the outside world the way Descartes treated it, as a separate domain quite apart from their consciousness. They omitted, or at least repressed, implications of their own awareness; and we are always astonished at the skill with which the object itself is *put there*. In consequence one Dutch still life looks a great deal like another. The painting does not change things. Only the objects offered us vary. Chardin's still life is different—for Chardin's pitchers, fruits, plates, and those imposing cloths dropping prudently over the edges of his tables are private meditations upon objects. This is what endows these things with their poetry—the poetry that is too often wanting in Dutch painting. For Chardin is bringing to bear upon them his own generous awareness; he is not canceling out the *way* he sees them. These utensils exist in an atmosphere we seldom feel in Dutch still lifes: we know that these things are being looked at. Do not the things almost seem to know they are being looked at? Chardin is quietly intimating to us that he sees them *thus*. The Dutch still life treats the world as given; Chardin, like his great follower Cézanne, treats the world as *taken*. The still life by Chardin or Cézanne is painting in which the object sustains the impact of a temperament, and the painting is a mode of contemplation. Cézanne's regard is more imperative and imperious. The simple object cannot resist it so well. But it assumes great dignity because it is looked at with a calm, tolerant vision that searches into its mystery.

I am not saying that either Chardin or Cézanne is a romantic; they are realists who draw the object back into the orbit of human reflection. As usual Baudelaire gives us the key to such problems when he says that romanticism is not a choice of subject but a way of looking at reality from within. In sum, romanticism, and modern painting generally, are belated replies to Descartes, bringing the outside world into profound contact with the self. Degas was no romantic, but his studies of ballet dancers show how the world, after romanticism, could be surprised from an unexpected angle—one's own, always.

What does all this mean for the authenticity of nineteenth-century painting? For one thing it means accented individuality, painting without official style but with a wide range of personal attempts to represent what appears when very different minds are directed toward the realm we call nature. Impressionism was, like realism, one aspect of the larger romantic effort to show how we are conscious of being conscious.

Generally speaking, the romantic painter illustrated what Schopenhauer had claimed philosophically: that for each of us the world is not a sun or an earth but, instead, an eye that sees the sun and a hand that feels the earth, making the world about us our idea of the world. Turner is among the romantic painters who represent the world as a form of consciousness—which is romanticism in a phrase. Turner's methods trace back to Claude's use of light and color; but Turner's vision is more subjective than Claude's. Turner is the British counterpart of Delacroix, and what Baudelaire wrote of Delacroix he might have written of Turner. The painter, Baudelaire says, must create another world of his own, which Baudelaire calls the New: "The true artist, the true poet, should only paint in accordance with what he sees and with what he feels." Then he gains his harmony— the harmony of Turner's evaporating vision, a "rich, joyful, or melancholy impression upon the soul," making the painter a hypnotist, as if he could project thought at a distance. Baudelaire said that Delacroix's color "thinks for itself" apart from the object it clothes. It is as abstract as thoughts can be, and reminds us again that the romantic painter represents the world as his consciousness of the world.

Romanticism is, then, a reaction against the dehumanizing of the world by Descartes and seventeenth-century science, which left the universe as a mechanical system in which man was a stranger. The romantics reintroduced into art a homocentric principle that had disappeared at the decline of the renaissance—not only homocentric, but *psychocentric*. Or we may take romantic painting as a form of laissez faire in art. But unlike liberalism in politics or economics, romantic painting was not burdened with ideologies. Instead, its freedom was "pure"—a freedom of consciousness.

This belief that reality is for us our awareness of reality explains why it is so hard to draw together the many painters in the romantic tradition; for romantic painting is only a record of the differing perceptions brought to bear upon the world, each authentic. If nineteenth-century painting lacks a canon, it does so because it was an affirmation of private perspectives, each perspective a deviation from absolutes that had too long been honored. Thus romanticism in painting has two contradictory aspects: a negative aspect of revolt against conventions, and a positive aspect of many private views of the world, each a mastering of reality. The latter aspect concerns us, the aspect that caused Ortega y Gasset to call the whole of modern painting a "retraction" from the object toward the painter: "The artist starting from the world about him, ends by withdrawing into himself." Modern painting is a form of "perspectivism" because the artist uses things as a point of departure for his own experience. The meanings of reality are enriched in direct ratio to the number of perspectives that are imposed upon the world; the world is continually being reconstructed by the perceptions interacting with it.

Alfred North Whitehead has pointed out the significance of the romantic reaction against the realm of mathematics that had been erected by "the century of genius," which conceived the Newtonian world order, a system of bodies moving in space by unalterable laws of force. This beautiful tidy mechanism had gone too far in excluding subjective experiences, and had alienated the human spirit from the domain of things. It had stripped the world of private values. The romantic reaction was the re-entry of these private values into the world, reading poetry back into the universe, permeating nature with human meanings. Whitehead rightly says that at the height of his powers Wordsworth "grasps the whole of nature as involved in the tonality of the particular instance." This particular tonality is Baudelaire's harmony. The romantic self heroically involved the whole world in the experience of the moment. Keats, for instance, looks at the Elgin Marbles, and as he does so the whole of Greek history, art, and even geography is enveloped in a vision saturated with the poet's

> . . . dizzy pain
> That mingles Grecian grandeur with the rude
> Wasting of old Time—with a billowy main—
> A sun—a shadow of a magnitude.
> ("*On Seeing the Elgin Marbles*")

So also alpine peaks are to Wordsworth "types and symbols of Eternity." The romantic artist feels that the world depends upon the consciousness of the percipient, and the present sensation takes on values that are much larger than the sensation itself. As Whitehead says, for the romantic artist "every spatio-temporal standpoint mirrors the world." The universe is saturated with a temperament.

Géricault is one of the "imperialistic" temperaments whose

work has atmosphere—an atmosphere of death and danger, the restlessness by which life consumes itself. He experimented with "grand" and "little" styles; but the restlessness remains as the signature of his temperament. Not his composition but his "touch" is the guarantee of the authenticity of his vision.

II

This question of touch is crucial, for the romantic painter's touch is a sign that he has entered into his own relation with the world. In *Les Voix du Silence* Malraux remarked that the appearance of personal touch marks the point at which academic painting collapsed, leaving us with only the "small change" of absolutes. This is not a calamity, for the painter's touch is proof that he has possessed the world for his own.

Each great painter of the period has his own touch. In many cases—notably in Delacroix and Corot—the touch varies from painting to painting, so that their work is a study of the many ways of possessing reality: a constant play of personality against the world. If we judged only by its subject, we should say that Delacroix's *Corner of the Studio* was painted by one of the Dutch little masters. But nobody would take it for Dutch because of the impatient touch, the intrusion of a personality getting between us and the corner of this room. When the Dutch treated these motifs, they excluded themselves as far as they could; they have a magic of the hand, but not a touch like that of Delacroix, who makes his hand the vehicle of his temperament, magnetizing this little region of actuality.

How completely unlike Delacroix's touch is Ingres' touch in *Le Bain Turc*. At first glance we say this work does not belong in the romantic tradition, and according to art history Ingres' "neo-classic" manner is opposed to Delacroix's "romanticism." But look again: is not Ingres' temperament in his touch? His repressed nature speaks through these congealed bodies, just as the ardent and outgoing nature of Delacroix speaks through the corner of his studio. These paintings assure us that the differences within nineteenth-century art are more radical than that between so-called classicism and so-called romanticism.

The genuine difference is between those who were painters and those who were illustrators—mere fashionable craftsmen. The romantics were not illustrators; nor was Ingres. The illustrators set down literary anecdotes, told a story. They were intent upon reporting an episode; their world was given to them before they began to paint; they did not have to invent it, to earn it—they needed only to move in. The illustrator did not care about his own personal relation to the scene; he did not have his own way of seeing it. He was primarily interested in what was happening in a world where everybody lives. Nobody but Ingres lives in the world of *Le Bain Turc*. Such painting is not illustration any more than is the corner of Delacroix's studio.

But J. L. E. Meissonier's accurate scenes from Napoleonic history are illustration. They are recorded with a skill that is distracting; they are a kind of Kodachrome photography. Meissonier has a hand that reports without touching. Baudelaire need not have worried so much about photography's killing art, for none of the authentic painters succumbed to it. *Le Bain Turc* is by no means photography; in spite of—or rather *because* of—its clear definition it is a sign of a troubled, compulsive temperament which can be called classic if you please: but classic in only a trivial sense. Ingres has his own touch, hard and arrogant; and these writhing nudes are his own dream, quite unlike what would be seen in any harem.

The instability of the romantic temperament is in the changeable touch of a painter like Delacroix. His splendid *Massacre at Scio* is in the baroque tradition of Rubens; but its poetry is Delacroix's own. We know that before he painted the *Massacre* he saw, in the salon of 1824, some landscapes by Constable—landscapes filled with English climate, he said. The result is that the atmosphere of the *Massacre* is undoubtedly romantic, as Rubens' full-blooded language is not. The difference between this painting and a Rubens is that Rubens' figures, resplendent as they are, do not exist in a local climate. Delacroix's figures exist in a quality of light and air pervading the whole composition. The *Massacre* is an oriental dream, and the dreamlike climate is heightened in *Roger and Angelica*, a romantic version of Claude and Rubens. The same atmosphere—with the romantic impulse of life to prey on itself—reappears in Delacroix's North African scenes like *Arab Horses Fighting in a Stable*, or in his *Lion Hunt*, with a driving rhythm that carries over into the wild motion of Van Gogh's hand or the organic flow of Renoir's brushwork. This mystique of power, making life a struggle, is also in the troubled touch of Géricault.

Romantic painting is filled with contradictions because the painter's feelings change, and the authenticity of this painting is inherent in these inconsistencies. Quite as obviously as romantic poets, romantic painters express the contradictory visions of life that might be called existential, since it was the existentialist Kierkegaard who said, "Opposites are reconciled in *me*." Romantic painting uses a logic of the self, not the logic of academic formulas; it has the logic of private experience, not of style.

We see little to link *Arab Horses Fighting* or any *Lion Hunt* with the Delacroix who painted the bleak nude called *Mlle. Rose*, which might be taken for the work of some realist like Eakins. How different this figure is from the nudes of Ingres, which are no less ascetic. How could the painter of those voluptuous nudes in the *Death of Sardanapalus* have done this study, a notation stripped of all we expect of the romantic imagination? It is nearly a travesty of the idealism we say is romantic.

This idealism takes form in Ingres, who is that strange contradiction we call the romantic rationalist. Ingres' metallic line, his bleached color, his lithographic clarity make his portrait of *Mme. de la Rivière* almost an abstraction. The portrait, hard as a cameo, is as personal a treatment as anything in Delacroix; his consciousness of the model is as finely cut as the rationalism of some of Shelley's chiseled verses:

> When the lamp is shattered,
> The light in the dust lies dead;
> When the cloud is scattered,
> The rainbow's glory is shed.
> When the lute is broken,
> Sweet tones are remembered not.
> When the lips have spoken,
> Loved accents are soon forgot.
> ("*Lines,*" 1822)

There is a note of cynicism in these verses and in the cold lucid figure of Mme. de la Rivière, who is reasoned into being as a presence *postulated* by decorative necessity. Or there is the more gracious presence of Ingres' friend Granet, whose portrait is surprisingly unlike that of Mme. de la Rivière. The remote calm vision of Granet has little decorative geometry; instead, the inspiration seems to be architectural, and the composition, very broad, is like some late-renaissance academic painting—perhaps landscapes by Domenichino or Poussin. Although this portrait is as abstract as the portrait of Mme. de la Rivière, the abstraction is in a different mode—for this painting is meditated rather than reasoned, if one may make this distinction. Granet exists in his own serene atmosphere, as dreamlike in its way as the atmosphere in Delacroix. But this is a classic dream, when the mind is in equilibrium, and in full command of very imposing structures.

Thus we note another contradiction, for the half-academic vision of Granet is more private than the huge impulsive

Raft of the Medusa painted by one of the volatile romantics, Géricault, who, like Delacroix in his famous *Liberty Leading the People*, sometimes resorted to journalism. To know the quieter, more inward Géricault, we must turn to his subtle, disturbing studies of the insane—the head of *La Folle*, where we are impressed not by what is said but by what cannot be said. This work brings not only the painter but also the beholder into a relation with the world that is truly psychic. Nothing could better prove that artists like Géricault discovered the unconscious long before Freud, or even Charcot. Goya is also profoundly romantic in his cruel understanding of life devouring itself inwardly as well as publicly. Psychoanalysis is merely an extension of the romantic discovery of man's consciousness of himself. Freud brings romanticism into modern science.

Nowhere is touch more decisive than in landscape painting, and to see how the self penetrated nature, we may glance at Constable and Corot, between whom there is a deep agreement. Both are forerunners of Cézanne, who late in the century made one of the most powerful private attacks on the outside world. Constable's analytic vision of Wivenhoe Park has little of the dream, for it is achieved at full consciousness, like Cézanne's attack on Montagne Sainte-Victoire. Constable realized the play of light almost as Cézanne grasped, as if by his hand, the planes of the mountain he so often studied. The miniature scale of Constable's scene does not deceive us: the activity of mind and sculpturesque touch that made this statement are as cogent as anything in early cubist painting. Ingres never carved in Constable's rough way—a carving that recalls the strongly hewn statues of the aging Michelangelo. Ingres slipped along the clear geometric curve of his figures, but he never worked inside their mass as Constable's brush did. Strangely enough, Ingres does his chiseling in a fluid medium, thinner than Constable's.

The scene at Wivenhoe Park is as "classic" as Corot's

Italian landscapes, his *View of Volterra*, for instance, which gives to an academic theme a romantic impatience and freedom. We can feel behind this dense atmosphere, where all is formally stated, a pressure of vision that never disturbed the late-baroque landscapes of Nicolas Poussin, who also went to Italy to find his style. Like Constable, Corot works in two or three different manners. There is this masterly Italian vision, holding everything in sculptural order. Then, just as Constable saw Salisbury Cathedral in an evening mist, shimmering under a gentle sky, Corot saw the Forest of Fontainebleau at an idyllic distance, blurred in the vapors from which his nymphs emerge. There is another Corot, too, who turns to the commonplace scenes he shares with Millet—Millet the painter of humble and rustic life, like Wordsworth casting atmosphere over the peasant's unre-membered tasks. This is the Millet who is a submerged romantic, an artist incapable of revolt: for behind Millet's vision of the French peasant is an almost stupid acceptance of things as they are—an acceptance quite at odds with the revolutionary spirit of most romantic painters. The Millet who accepts is often akin to Courbet.

This may sound like a strange opinion, since Courbet is said to be the rebel, the republican, the socialist. Yet Courbet often performs in the same spirit and with the same touch as Millet. His *Stonebreakers* toil with the resignation of Millet's peasants. Besides, Courbet is a link between Millet's somber pastoral atmosphere and the proletarian art with which Van Gogh began in the Borinage. In his wood-land scenes—*The Edge of the Forest*, that great green symphony—Courbet mediates between Constable and Cé-zanne. The same memorable atmosphere fills the great *Atelier du Peintre*, which Courbet intended to be a social manifesto. This pretentious aim simply goes to show how artists can misunderstand their own work; for this composi-tion is a majestic world as strange and magical as anything the romantics dreamed. It has a brooding orchestral quality, a tonality significant in a painter like Courbet, for it brings us back to Baudelaire with his notion that a painting must have a private resonance. Hegel pointed out that romantic art passes beyond classic form to gain what he calls spirituality. Romantic art, he remarks, abandons the external world to take refuge within the self. The romantic painter no longer wished to present images from the outside world only. Instead, his spirit imbued the world, changing its features and transcending its objects.

Among the painters who suggest how thoroughly the world was transformed by romantic consciousness is the little-known Adolphe J. T. Monticelli, whose visions of nature and of fêtes have a haunting air of what is dreamed rather than what is seen. His darkling self-indulgent work is as deeply scored as the harmonies in Gauguin, who sought his dream in Tahiti. For romantic painting eventually led to Gauguin, an artist who hovers between what is within and what is without, and who shows how nineteenth-century painting achieved a dominion of temperament over things. Gauguin recapitulates the whole romantic achievement: the wealthy color of Delacroix, the abstract line of Ingres, the dreamlike scale of late impressionist palette, but above all the private touch, the personal vision. Such a vision was also reached by Van Gogh and Cézanne, and all three were working at the height of their powers in the 1880's.

The date is significant, as Fritz Novotny notes, because the century between Kant's *Critique of Pure Reason*, finished in 1780, and the post-impressionist painting of the 1880's is the time when the revolutionary artist turned away from conventional academic painting to seek new perceptions, to see authentically. Romantic painting was indeed nature seen through a temperament. It put man at the center again.

To see things authentically was not a problem for most artists of preceding eras. It was not a problem for the romanesque or gothic artist, who did not have to worry about the authenticity of his work or carry the burden of the self into his shop. But like certain renaissance or mannerist painters, the romantic painter was always troubled, as well as inspired, by his need to have his own perception. The need for personal vision accounts for "the lack of uniformity" in nineteenth-century painting, its "fragmentary nature and many-sidedness." Novotny probably misses the implications of the romantic revolt when he says that the nineteenth century was dominated by naturalism. Beyond question the bulk of this painting was naturalistic—even photographic. But the bulk of nineteenth-century painting does not matter much. The significant minority of painters treated nature as a reflex of the self, bringing their consciousness directly to bear upon the world.

Romantic painting went on until the cubists, following Cézanne, attempted to think through the problem of man's relation to the world in a new way. Cubism was theoretical; romantic painting was not. The cubists were impersonal as the romantic painters were not. Systematically the cubists restudied how consciousness deals with the actualities outside consciousness; and in so doing they ended romanticism. And after cubism came new experiments.

But Hegel was right: romantic art approaches the condition of music. And Baudelaire was right: romantic painting is the equivalent of the dream that begot it, brought into being like a private world. This was not the world where we live every day. Turner's excitable vision proves that, as well as Gauguin's melodious peace. It is a representation of a world that is our consciousness of the world.

Existence and Entropy

I

As one of the great philosophers of romanticism Hegel believed that during the course of history man's spirit frees itself from matter until it triumphantly dominates the world. Henri Bergson is the philosopher of a revised romanticism concerned not with a quest for freedom but with the difficulty of finding where an authentic self resides. In his effort to "touch bottom," Bergson turns inward to contemplate how the self exists within the flow of time, how it endures behind or within change. He devotes himself to the theme of our buried life inaccessible to reason, the existence that dissolves the self into a mobility of consciousness—a consciousness almost unconscious, having only a direction or a submerged duration, not an heroic or evident identity. If the self is to be known, it must be intuited in the dim and quiet eddies streaming like quicksands far below the mechanism of the rational mind, which is forever falsifying our experience by its clear and intelligible logic. Bergson does not attempt to impose the self upon the world, or even to escape from the world, but to plumb the existence that is instinctual, fluid, and inexpressible, the silent existence that annuls thought and seems to be a diffusion of the person rather than a definition of the person. In spite of the romantic strains in Bergson, he presides at the liquidation of the imperious romantic self, a liquidation that has been increasingly rapid as the twentieth century overtakes us.

According to Bergson the self does endure; but any image of the self gives it a fixed contour that is only an artifact. Therefore Bergson amends the idealism of Shelley and Carlyle, who tried to give the self an identity by their romantic rationalism. Bergson insists that reason makes dupes of us by reducing experience to ideas that are abstractions. Since the self is an endless change of sensibility, the authentic selfhood can only be lived, not thought; our real existence must be sought in the shifting currents of our most immediate consciousness. Any other formula for the self is merely put on, like ready-made clothes that do not fit. To think of one's self as having a single clear identity is to translate our existence into a mere logical reconstruction, to transpose the data of experience into concepts that are extraneous to the data themselves.

Bergson agrees with the empiricists who take one's "personality" to be merely synthetic as soon as it is thought or defined, since what we call personality is an aspect of the many psychic states through which we are constantly passing. The self that can be thought is an impersonal self, a diagram of someone who is dissembled. Bergson places mathematics at the opposite pole from the self, for mathematical reasoning is an attempt to substitute the ready-made for the being-made. Consequently Bergson is more sympathetic to biology than to mathematics, and his subjectivity is more sensitive to evolution than the subjectivity of earlier romantic thinkers who were so intent on the absolutes they took for eternal truths.

In the same way the subjectivity of Proust's novel is subtler, more finely nuanced, than the subjectivity of most romantic writers. Yet Proust remains romantic in essence, convinced, like Bergson, that the self lives amid a stream of inward experience in a sort of time not to be measured by the clock. This subjective time, into which Wordsworth had once plunged, is known only by the intensity of one's feeling and is purely qualitative, not quantitative. Bergson calls it duration, not time; it is time translated into psychic relations, time penetrated by the intuitions that reveal to us the essence of our existence amid a world of sensations furnished by our encounter with things, people, events. It is time distilled by consciousness.

By making his novel a study of "pure" consciousness, Proust refines the romantic notion of selfhood, dissolving the personality into the most tentative feelings and impressions until it seems to be only a mirage. At the opposite pole from nineteenth-century realists, Proust renounces the solid world of objects and explores the constantly thinning fringe of contact between things and the sensations of things fading off into a penumbra of intimations which is all that is left of the romantic self: "When I saw any external object, my consciousness that I was seeing it would remain between me and it, enclosing it in a slender, incorporeal outline which prevented me from ever coming directly in contact with the material form; for it would volatilize itself in some way before I could touch it." That other belated and somber romantic novelist Conrad puts the same filter of consciousness between himself and the events he tells; for as Marlow sits brooding in the darkness falling over the lower reaches of the Thames, he says that his adventure with Kurtz was like a dream: "To him the meaning of an episode was not inside, like a kernel, but outside, enveloping the tale which brought it out only as a glow brings out a haze, in the likeness of those misty halos that sometimes are made visible by the spectral illumination of moonshine." Like Conrad, Proust is convinced that "a literature which is content with 'describing things,' with offering a wretched summary of their lines and surfaces, is, in spite of its pretension to realism, the furthest from reality, the one which impoverishes us and saddens us the most." For Proust and Conrad reality is a passage between states or perceptions so private they can only be suggested. So our genuine experiences reduce themselves to "multiple and varied sensations" that are fugitive and incommunicable. The self tends to vanish behind these fluctuating sensations.

The phrase reminds us that during the 1920's Eliot was saying a good deal about our incoherent responses to life; or as Robert Musil put it, "These days one never sees oneself whole and one never moves as a whole." Musil is inclined to accept this incoherence as a condition of modern life. Eliot, however, evidently was still hoping, like the romantics, that we might find some integral self behind our dissociated responses, and he yearned to find it. Hermann Hesse in his allegorical novel *Steppenwolf* went further than either Eliot or Musil in examining our disintegrating selves, rejecting any romantic faith that the self can have an identity. In fact, Hesse called it an error to presume that one has identity—each is only a collection of conflicting selves. He names this condition madness—that is, "the separation of the unity of the personality into these numerous pieces." Taking this schizoid state as a basis for a contemporary psychology, Hesse says we can rearrange the pieces of the self into many mirror-like changing patterns, and after our soul has fallen apart, we can make a large number of surprising moves in the game of life. Our personality is an illusion. The romantic quest of the self has ended in schizophrenia.

There are sinister implications in this novel because Hesse is referring to a madness that has afflicted the Germans, whose recent history exhibits the abominations that occur when man has no steady vision of his own nature. The Germans have not had this vision—which is one reason why they have been intoxicated by Wagnerian music expressing a blind urge toward destiny. "The German intellectual has constantly rebelled against the word and against reason and courted music," Hesse remarks. He is repeating what Nietzsche wrote in *The Birth of Tragedy from the Spirit of Music:* "Music alone allows us to understand the delight felt at the annihilation of the individual." Adrian Leverkuehn, the hero of Thomas Mann's new Faustus legend, has given himself over to Dionysiac music. The spectacle is doubly intimidating because the romantic titanism persists even after the romantic self has collapsed into a schizophrenic state, which produces both crime and art. Nietzsche was close enough to the glory of romantic ideals still to believe that his Dionysiac heroism would be redemptive. Mann and Hesse know it is not.

Outside Germany the self did not fall to pieces on a national scale—or perhaps we could say that disintegrating the self did not become an official national program. Nevertheless the self did fall to pieces elsewhere. Ford Madox Ford wrote about the unreliability of the modern self in a novel he originally named *The Saddest Story*—which would have been a better title than *The Good Soldier.* By means of a technical trick confining the narrative to a single naïve point of view, Ford is able to expose the duplicity of each of his characters, "normal" though they appear—Edward Ashburnham, who is a genteel rake and a half-tragic victim; Leonora Ashburnham, who is a kind of devout procuress and a martyr; Nancy Rufford, who is a moral fury and a faded Eve; and Florence, a degenerate Cleopatra able to keep up appearances of a sort. Technically the novel is an exercise like cubist painting, which treated its subjects by seeing them from contrary points of view simultaneously. But ethically Ford is passing judgment on the modern self in its state of decomposition, a state partly due to the loss of any effectual codes.

Accounts of the disintegrated self are everywhere in our literature. The breakdown seems complete in a work like Paul Bowles' *The Sheltering Sky*, where Kit and Port Moresby deliberately vacate their place in American society and, following the path of Kurtz into the heart of Africa, discard even the memory of civilization as they go deeper into the Sahara until they are lost—lost to recognition of themselves, lost in a waste land that presents only the dry contours of our modern geography. They abdicate through fear as well as anxiety; they wish to discard themselves along with their luggage. When Kit reaches the great silence of the desert and enters the harem, she feels safe and calm; she opens her little valise and watches the small white handkerchiefs and the scissors as they fall out. "Then she handled them absently; they were like the fascinating and mysterious objects left by a vanished civilization." Kit chooses to go to the end of the line, and to stay there.

Bowles strikes the note of "decadence" more audibly than Hemingway, whose lifelong safari was also a way of abdicating, and whose big-game hunting was a symptom of consuming weariness. The "Alexandrian" theme is elaborately worked up in Durrell's tetralogy, which devotes itself to the thesis that even the force of love cannot give coherence to the modern self; for in the heat of sexual union we are always embracing someone else who is not there. Durrell wryly uses as one of his epigraphs a passage from Freud's letters to the effect that four persons are involved in every sexual act, and in so quoting Freud he ironically rejects the idea of passion that was supposed to give purpose, unity, and direction to the life of the romantic hero. The character of Pursewarden serves, it would seem, as Durrell's mouthpiece when he asks, "Are people continuously themselves, or simply over and over again so fast that they give the illusion of continuous features—the temporal flicker of old silent film?" In the opiate-like atmosphere of Alexandria nobody has a personality—but only changing relations with others as figures rotate about each other.

Early in the twentieth century Gide, that diabolic man of letters, remarked that the self is capable of anything. He implied that the romantic quest for sincerity—the finding of the real self—is a ridiculous venture. For as he discovered, if you remove the pressure of the usual codes even for an instant, we are capable of every sort of irrational, unexpected act—even of crime and other forms of gratuitous behavior. The whole question of sincerity vexed Gide, since he was inclined to revise himself every moment, and nothing was more different from himself than himself. This is Montaigne's old renaissance theme of the diversity of the self; but Gide was interested in nothing except what was irregular. He reached the extreme point of an inquiry Stendhal had made: Where is the true self behind the roles one can play? Stendhal thought of the novel as a mirror of the conflicting facets of life seen from a high road. Gide makes the refraction more shattering; he thinks an admirable subject for a novel would be the "decrystallization" of love between a husband and a wife after fifteen years of marriage, the husband discovering what he really is only after he ceases to love his wife. Stendhal thought of love as a constant crystallization and decrystallization. Gide offers us only the decrystallizing phase. He goes so far as to object to characters acting as one expects them to, for any consistency proves they are artificial. Gide bases his characters on the discontinuity principle.

Conrad was less perverse than Gide, but was also able to dismantle the Western self. Kurtz, the apostle of civilization, is able to abandon himself to every horror imaginable at the heart of darkness, which is in himself, not in the Congo. The wilderness whispered to Kurtz things he could not have believed in Europe; and he was fascinated. As Marlow listens to the drums beating in the night, he is not sure whether it is the throbbing of his own heart; he is loyal to Kurtz because he knows that Kurtz is his alter ego with an instinct for degradation. Dostoevsky was already able to bisect the civilized self. There is the thinnest of barriers between Myshkin the saint and his criminal self, his alter ego Rogojin the murderer. The barrier is broken when the two, who are one, lie on each side of the murdered Nastasia: "Listen—tell me—how did you?—with a knife?" *Letters from the Underworld* is a nearly clinical report of the fracturing of a self: "A man loves to act as he *likes*, and not necessarily as reason and self-interest would have him do. Yes, he will even act straight against his interests." Dostoevsky was convinced that the middle-class self did not always behave as the economists supposed it did; sometimes the prudent will recklessly disregard their calculation. Two plus two make four when we are dealing with things; but two plus two make five is a formula not without its attraction for human beings. So Dostoevsky upsets the rationalism of the liberal tradition. A rebel like Raskolnikov reasons his way to crime, and like Captain Ahab, throws overboard his charts and compasses. Now Samuel Beckett is telling us that we do not live until we try to divide twenty-two by seven.

For more than a century the rebel has insisted that existence is absurd, that man does not live authentically until he accepts the inexplicable. This is one of the central themes among the existentialists, who carry on a romantic quest for the self and its meaning. Like the immoralists of the nineteenth century, existentialists reaffirm the incompetence of reason or logic to explain, or even to guide, our deeply lived experiences. Kierkegaard, who led the nineteenth century from the problems of the romantic self to the existential problem of authenticity, saw that logic can deal with life only by mere approximations which never convincingly get at the crisis of the instant when the either/or choice is made. This choice is decided by imperatives before which reason is helpless. Reason can explain away the absurdity of the crisis, can mediate between either and or, can impose on the course of our life an intelligible meaning—whereupon the meaning is emptied out precisely because it has been defined.

The existential question is honesty: Kirkegaard, like Nietzsche, hated liars and hypocrites. He claimed "I was never like the others," which is another way of saying his life was implausible in a century devoted to plausibilites. He scorned institutional Christianity, or Christendom as he contemptuously called it; and like Nietzsche he was willing to reverse all accepted values in his thirst for truth.

The romantic quest for sincerity—for emotional authenticity—thus changes into an existential quest for a different kind of authenticity, a kind of confidence in the self while the self feels an earthquake underneath, while one has "nothing to hold on to" after fear and trembling have shaken the foundations of reason. The most agonizing question of all is whether one is deceiving one's self, whether one is using "bad faith," which is a tactic of evading, a willingness to tolerate sham. Carlyle's question, Who Am I? leads directly to Ortega's question, Is My Existence Authentic? Julien Sorel's doubt about his sincerity, his eagerness to find his real self, is followed by Kierkegaard's anxiety to be sure he is a Christian: Is his faith, which is rationally absurd, held fast with a passionate inwardness that is inviolable? Ortega says that we do not begin to live until we feel ourselves lost—that is, until we feel the security of logic give way and we try to get along with only probabilities, or possibilities, which reason cannot completely master. In true existence every instant brings uncertainty. A man sits in his room and decides to take a walk. When he opens his door to go out, he assumes the street is still there. It probably is there; he must believe it is there; he cannot think it is there unless he makes some assumptions. To allow this uncertainty is to exist, to live immediately and intimately with the texture of the human condition in the foreground. The self must come to terms with an undependable world. But we must behave as if we were sure. Ortega calls reason a brief zone of clarity waning on both sides to darkness.

The existentialists who have most passionately sought authenticity have assumed that the self has an identity. As Sartre says, there is no exit from the hot chamber in which we are confined when we come face to face with ourselves. The self is imprisoned inside our skins for life. The existentialists have believed the self to be *there*. It may be irrational, divided, baffled, fearful, torn by doubt—but it exists; we ourselves make it while we choose this or that as we meet the possibilities of each instant. The existentialists are convinced that we choose; and there is somebody to make the choice, even if it be wrong or made in bad faith. Each one reaches his own fate—which is to say each one attains selfhood. When the existentialist says "You are your life," he confirms our responsibility for being what we are.

II

Existentialism has been complicated and qualified by a post-existentialist literature and painting where another question is implicit: How if the self has only an uncertain existence? How if the self that chooses is one more figment? Suppose its existence is entirely contingent? This phase of post-existential thought appears when Jean Grenier remarks apropos of "brutal" painting that we now walk in a universe where there is no longer an echo of the "I." In so saying Grenier presses to an extreme the dilemma of men without qualities: their experiences are no longer their own, in a more radical sense than Musil guessed. Our *situation*—the field in which our experiences happen to us, if they be our experiences at all—seems to be more actual than the self on which these experiences are imposed.

How, then, can we describe experience without a self on

which to pivot this experience? This question gives existentialism another cast. What does experience mean after the self has been diminished or, perhaps, has vanished? It is a question that occurs to Eddie in Elizabeth Bowen's *Death of the Heart*: Eddie says he was sure he was himself simply because he was nobody else. Eddie's self is what is left after the others have been subtracted. But suppose we cannot even subtract the others, who also have no selves? We are subtracting a missing value from a missing value. According to the old logic, multiplying a minus by a minus gave a plus. No longer. Such logic has broken down not only in mathematics but also in post-existentialist speculations upon the human condition. The difficulty is the more bewildering because after all the identities, or possible identities, of the self are subtracted, there seems to remain some existence, however minimal—some residue of a self that still causes us trouble, malaise, unhappiness. This minimal self, a nearly spectral identity that refuses to vanish, or that cannot vanish, is the cornerstone on which a new humanism must be based—a humanism so strange it seems not to be humanistic.

In any case this is a problem facing writers of a-literature, with characters who are anti-heroes appearing in fictions known as the anti-novel, dramas known as anti-theater, and, I presume, if we include Allen Ginsberg, poems that are anti-poetry. This kind of writing is aptly called a scuttling of literature. It is also the scuttling of a humanism that persisted in existential self-centeredness.

As everyone recognizes, the scuttling of literature started a century ago. Verlaine wanted to take eloquence and wring its neck; after the poem became music, all the rest was literature. The nonsense written by Lewis Carroll is anti-poetry; and in our day Eliot once wrote that the "poetry does not matter" since words slip, crack, and perish, always in different kinds of failure. The anti-drama was full blown in Alfred Jarry's *Ubu Roi*; and Strindberg's *Dream Play* proved by a logic of discontinuity that "anything can happen" to characters with a "slight groundwork of reality," for they can "split, double, and multiply. They evaporate, crystallize, scatter and converge" in a plot "without law." This improvising went further in Pirandello, who analyzed and often demolished the conventions of the well-made play. The anti-novel appeared as far back as Sterne's *Tristram Shandy* (1760-67)—if it had not already appeared in Cervantes—and the so-called realists sometimes wrote a kind of anti-literature. Flaubert's *Bouvard and Pécuchet* is an instance; and *Sentimental Education* is an early anti-novel with an anti-hero. The demolition of conventional fiction was hastened by stream-of-consciousness, used in Edouard Dujardin's *Les Lauriers Sont Coupés* (1887). One can trace a whole tradition of anti-literature.

Meanwhile Nietzsche was creating a sort of anti-philosophy, putting reason in the service of the will and leaping beyond the confines of logic to free the spirit of man. Nietzsche shook to its foundation the systematic thought of the century when he stated that "a culture based on the principles of science must be destroyed when it begins to grow illogical—that is, to retreat before its own conclusions." Both literature and science were forced to retreat before their own conclusions until a rout was imminent: Rimbaud intended his work to be one way of assassinating poetry, and Whitehead saw how the mechanistic science of the age could not dislodge the conviction that man is a self-determining organism. The radical inconsistency between ideas of freedom and ideas of determinism gives a destructive tone to Hardy's *Jude the Obscure*, which in temper, if not in technique, is an anti-novel savage in its hostility to man and also to the laws of nature.

In France the impressionists invented their own sort of anti-painting, promptly condemned as the ruination of art. The academic palette broke up, and brushwork at last turned barbaric among the fauves, who successfully demonstrated that painting can precede thinking. Much of this revolt from "art" and literature took the guise of immoralism, decadence, or primitivism. The sabotage of reason, painting, and poetry continued after the First World War in the antics of Dada and surrealism. Anti-painting and anti-literature are not new.

Yet the subversion of art now in progress is not like these half-romantic subversions, which were almost an act of insolence against convention and society. Many of the writers, especially, were rebels in the nineteenth-century manner, holding to a principle announced by Nechaev when he addressed a generation of Russian assassins: "Our task is universal, total, and final destruction." The nihilist, even in literature, was a variety of terrorist. But terrorism is a form of irritated individuality—one man against the world, embarked headlong on a course Marx sneeringly called a Robinsonade, man playing a Promethean role he could not bring himself to discard until the war to make a world safe for democracy caused many to say goodbye to all that.

It took Hiroshima and the concentration camps to ruin once for all this Promethean image of man. The destruction was so total during and after the Second World War that art went down with everything else; and as Czeslaw Milosz remarks, we have almost no literature of modern frightfulness because the artist was overborne by the scale of the calamity. We have lived through gigantic disasters, but they do not seem to be ours. To write about them would be a romantic luxury; we are struck dumb before such catastrophe. Our need is not to seek a self—much less to assert a self—but to get out from under a self, to escape from a heavy burden of freedom. It is perhaps more than this: we want to get beyond the self, beyond personality. T. S. Eliot must have felt a need for some such disburdening when he noted that the poet must escape from his personality in his verse, not exploit his personality.

The urge to be rid of the last heroisms of the romantic self is partly due to the terror we have seen; but it is also due to an absorption of the self into the culture-media of our world. Again the character of Ulrich in Musil's novel speaks for the moderns as he speculates on his own negative form of existence, and accounts for his lack of responsibility by saying, "There has arisen a world of qualities without a man to them, of experiences without anyone to experience them, and it almost looks as though . . . the comforting weight of personal responsibility would dissolve into a system for formulae for potential meanings." For his part the "dissolution of the anthropocentric attitude has finally begun to affect the personality itself; for the belief that the most important thing about experience is the experiencing of it, and about deeds the doing of them, is beginning to strike most people as naïve." Ulrich has a sense that the value of his actions depends not upon himself but upon "the whole complex to which they belonged." In his own eyes Ulrich does not *live*; instead he belongs to a system of relationships where everything that happens is a symbol for other happenings to be felt only as they bear upon still more remote happenings. Because of its unfocused meanings Ulrich's life seems "tiresome"; it is merely a function dependent on other functions whose significance levels off into distances and circumstances quite beyond his comprehension or concern. Ulrich sees himself as a trivial item in some vast equation of forces—the forces that tend, as he says, to run down into an average condition, a compromise, and inertia. "The events of people's lives have, after all, only to the least degree originated in them." By feeling so negligible, he is deprived of the assurances and safeguards Western man has had since the Greeks.

When man is alienated from his own experiences, psychology does not help. In a remark that has become a cliché Nathalie Sarraute has requested the novelist who hears the word psychology to lower his eyes and blush. In asking this Mme. Sarraute is once again proving that the artist feels what is happening before the rest of us feel it. We have turned to psychology as a means of dealing with our selves and with others. Much of this psychology is based upon the very poetic theory of Freud, who has mythologized our experience for us. Is it blasphemous to say that Mme. Sarraute is right and that Freud is wrong, that she has a better reading of today's self? The Freudian creed has taken nearly scholastic form precisely at an hour when the self has been canceled by the laws of large numbers.

Nobody has given us a nobler ethic than Freud, whose effort was to make the civilized self master of the barbaric self, whose aim as a scientist was to cleanse the Id, to let the Ego rule in its own house. But how if Freud was a belated romantic with a concept of the self that is no longer valid? How if the Ego be a romantic notion like Shelley's vision of Prometheus? Erich Fromm has suspected there is something wrong with Freudian theory, and tries to account for the new selflessness of modern man by saying that we are alienated from ourselves by our marketing orientation. The self, he says, becomes impersonal whenever it is looked upon as something to be exploited like a product on the market, like a sum to be invested. Then the person is identical only with his economic role, the role he plays in the open market along with other alienated selves, who are also saleable commodities. Or worse, our selves are identical with our roles as consumers whose desires must be immediately satisfied by products we buy to give us the status we wish. Since we do not need what we consume, even our satisfactions are alienated from the self. Thus we have projected the self into things, and have lost ourselves in worshiping idols of the market place.

III

Beyond doubt Fromm has cited one of the reasons for Ulrich's feeling that his life is a negligible part of a great social complex that does not matter to him. Ulrich says that his life is tiresome. Fromm says that man is dead. There is another aspect of this exhaustion, for the forces of the market, too, may tend toward a state of inertia. Physicists have had a good deal to say about entropy, a notion that is as anti-romantic as the marketing orientation. In effect entropy is the tendency of an ordered universe to go over into a state of disorder. This is another way of saying that the behavior of things tends to become increasingly random; and in any system tending toward the random there is a loss of direction. The universe as we have thought of it from Aristotle to Einstein was a system controlled by laws that produced a cosmos instead of a chaos—that is, the universe was highly structured; but entropy is a drift toward an unstructured state of equilibrium that is total.

The meaning of entropy is illustrated in Boltzmann's theory that with the passage of time there is a gradual transition in nature from the systematic to the random because the universe suffers a leveling of energy until all distinctions are obliterated. The natural order runs down, we say, like an unwound clock, losing its capacity to work. In classical physics it was presumed that the future is like the past, since there are uniform, continuing laws of energy by which things act and react. It is now argued, however, that this continuing operation of uniform laws would rob the future of its very meaning; for the future is not like the past or the present. The future is that in which time becomes effective; and the mark of time is the increasing disorder toward which our system tends.

The future is more random than the present or the past. Jacob Bronowski compares the future to a stream of gas shot from a nozzle: the farther the gas is propelled from the nozzle, the more random the motion of the molecules. The gas diffuses; it loses direction. Thus during the course of time entropy increases. Time can be measured by the loss of structure in our system, its tendency to sink back into that original chaos from which it may have emerged. Technically entropy is spoken of as a drift toward thermodynamical equilibrium—a squandering of energy into a permanent state where no observable events occur. Every isolated system increases in entropy until it reaches a condition of rest. One meaning of time is the drift toward inertia.

It is not hard to see what the theory of entropy does to the nineteenth-century ideal of progress, the far future as Tennyson hopefully called it, the wonder that is to be, and all other utopian visions on which the romantics and Victorians depended. Tennyson's Ulysses was a hero who believed that beyond the twilight there were always gleaming worlds. We seem to be moving toward no enchanted future, but toward a darkness from which comes no morning. Entropy is evolution in reverse.

More dismal still: the erasure of personality which exhausts Ulrich is a form of entropy in the social order. Age itself is entropy, and life is a form of negative entropy: a living organism wins its individuality by resisting a tendency to fade back into the stuff of dreams from which we are made and into which we seem, together with our great globe, destined to vanish. In the closing passages of Camus' *Stranger* Meursault has his own sort of bleak Prospero-vision when he feels cleansed of rebellion and emptied of all hope as he looks up at a dark sky still spangled with stars but signifying to him a benign indifference in a universe that has ceased to concern him. Meursault has done with the anger and contempt he felt for a while, and even with the automatism of his life among the others; he is willing to surrender to a cosmic neutrality. Before he goes to the guillotine Meursault has a Hamlet-like sense that the earth with its overhanging firmament is sterile, flat, weary, and unprofitable; but he can make his quietus because there will be no bad dreams after he has ceased to be. The destiny of man is obliteration, and our life is only a brief rebellion against the randomness into which things are ebbing. Unlike Hamlet, Meursault speaks prosaically; there is no poetry left in him or his universe. But in his barren and constrained prose he is able to hint at the force of the dark winds blowing against him from his future, and asks what difference it makes to him or to anybody. Meursault refuses any longer to swim upstream; he is willing to accept a fate that cancels out all heroism and overtakes him like a great fatigue. He succumbs to entropy.

Schopenhauer and the romantics told us that not to will is not to live. But to will is to expend the energy that enables us to resist drifting toward darkness. While we live, we succeed for a little while in freeing ourselves from the disorder we create by the very process of our living. Our life is a way of dissipating the forces that organize our system. There is a parallel to the theory of entropy in Schopenhauer himself, for his pessimism arose from his knowledge of the agony of willing, a striving that is incapable of any satisfaction. If, for a moment, the will attains its aim, then boredom sets in; and for the nineteenth century boredom was not, as Schopenhauer says, an evil to be lightly thought of, but "real despair." The only redemption from the torment of the will was to quench it, to silence it finally and utterly by a total resignation of the impulse to live. By such resignation we reduce the world to nothingness, for if our world is but a mirror of the self that wills it into being, then "to those in whom the will has turned and denied itself, this very real world of ours with all its suns and galaxies, is—nothing."

Under the guise of the death-wish Freud gave psychoanalysis its own version of the theory of entropy. If, he says, the tendency of instinct is toward repeating or restating an earlier condition, then the desire to return to the inorganic is irresistible, and our instinct is to obliterate the disturbance we call consciousness. "The organism is resolved to die in its own way," and the path of our life is simply our own way of choosing our progress toward death. The ultimate pleasure is an untroubled security of not-being;

therefore the drag toward inertia (Thanatos) is constantly behind that self-assertion which we call living. "The inanimate was there before the animate"—a wisdom graven ineffaceably, though illegibly, within the unconscious self. Like Schopenhauer or Nietzsche, Freud assumes that the root of all our troubles is our individuality, which we would extinguish.

As Sartre and the existentialists phrase it, the ground of our being is nothingness; and if nothingness is the support of our being, our true being is a heightened consciousness of the nothingness of our being. Our death is the crisis in our life. If we translate the theory of entropy into metaphysical language, we have something resembling the thought of Heidegger, for whom existence is a mode of standing-out, an EX-stasis. The standing-out of the self over a brief span of time is miraculous because the ultimate horizon of our being is nothingness; and if this is so, our authentic existence arises from seeing the self existing against the boundary of the future—the future that is really different from the present or the past, the future that gives time its desperate meaning. For the ultimate horizon of our future is our death. Heidegger assigns us an existence that is negative—negative in that it is *not* entropic. Our lives have meaning only in the perspective of our death, of our ceasing to be, of our extinction by entropy. In a more symbolic phrase Thomas Mann speaks of entropy by saying that death—nothingness—is not strange; life—our rebellion against nothingness—is strange, for life is merely a fever in matter.

Only against the horizon of one's death can one attain one's fate, which is unique for each because only our death is inalienably our own. Heidegger defines the self as the silence of a being before its own situation, into which it is "thrown" by no will of its own; and without having any choice whether to exist, we appear, then choose, then disappear. What freedom we have is reduced to a recognition that we are finite and doomed. There is an axiom in classical philosophy that from nothing, nothing is made: *ex nihilo nihil fit*. Heidegger revises this axiom to read: from Nothing all that is, is. In tragic guise Heidegger and Sartre give their sanction to the scientific notion of entropy: existence affirms itself in the face of nothingness, in the consciousness of its ultimate nothingness. On such terms it is hard to be romantic about the self.

Our recent literature—or a-literature—proves that romanticism is unnecessary. Further, it may prove that most preceding literature and art, like most preceding ethic, has been romantic in one way or another. A-literature implies that the humanism we inherited from the Greeks was too romantic. Perhaps we have lived through an era in thought and history more revolutionary than we have guessed. To the truly modern mind man appears in a perspective different from the perspective any former Western philosophy has given, different from any former perspective in Western art. This revolution troubles us, and justly, because it may be a final deromanticizing of man's view of himself; it suggests that any surviving humanism must be based upon a negative view of the self, if not a cancellation of the self. By this I mean a humanism that is not, to use Musil's term, anthropocentric. This displacement of man from the center is quite unlike the displacement of man by renaissance science; for that displacement was itself only a feat of man's own reason by which he explained the universe through new laws of his own devising, an exploit about which scientists now have grave doubts. And any such neutralizing of the self in the modern sense will require us to alter our notions of tragedy.

Is it thinkable that even our so-called classical views of man were also romantic? That in making men heroic in a classic way, they only disguised the romanticism by calling it tragic? When I say our perspective is unlike any perspective Western man has had, I hint that Eastern man has had another perspective, a perspective in many ways like the perspective-toward-nothingness in our notion of entropy and our existentialism. One of the reasons Zen has its hold on us is, obviously, that Eastern man has been able to surrender to nothingness more easily than Western man. The horizon of Eastern thought has always been more distant and indistinct than the horizon of Western thought, as the art of Sung and Tang periods shows; and Eastern man has been able to give himself to the drift of things, to nature, more selflessly than man in the West, tormented as he has been by an active will, the fever at the core of his being. The romantics called this fever *Weltschmerz*.

To be sure the Greeks did not run this romantic fever, for they had no clear notion of the will; yet they did believe that man determines his fate to the extent that he is answerable for the choices he makes. The Greeks were inclined to suppose with Aristotle that however passional the nature of man may be, he has the ability to decide (*Proairesis*), and that however his life may be subject to chance, misdirection, or misfortune, his tragic blunder is due to some error for which he is accountable. Only the gods are exempt from making this sort of blunder; or if they blunder, they are not liable to any moral law of retribution. The Greek tragic world was constructed by extending into the cosmos the moral laws of the *polis*, and according to these laws the tragic hero, as well as the political man, must try to make the right decision for the right reasons and with the right disposition or "character." Greek tragedy was humanistic in the sense that man had to assume responsibility for his choices, his blindness, his offenses against laws written in the heavens, laws that gave a moral structure to nature. Even Greek science was humanistic, or anthropomorphic, for the Greeks were able, happily, to exist in a limited, closed, provincial world that conformed to *Logos*. Just as the Greek tragic sense persisted in the background of drama until the present, so also the Greek *Logos* persisted through the whole era of renaissance science. But now the scientist and the artist have recognized, at almost the same instant, that we are walking in a universe where there is no echo of the "I." If our science is unlike past science, our literature—or anti-literature—is unlike past literature; and I suspect that our new perspective in literature comes to us along with a new perspective in science. Jacob Bronowski has remarked that crucial periods in literature have often coincided with crucial periods in science.

IV

To show how deeply we have revised our science, we must consider that the very notions of cause and effect—the premises of the old science—have been qualified. Bronowski says that the three notions science accepted from Aristotle were the idea of order, the idea of cause and effect, and the idea of chance. The idea of order was based upon the idea of cause and effect; and chance was what could not be explained by cause and effect. Thus the logical structures of the human mind were laid upon the universe, which was still a provincial area for the exercise of *Logos*. The late Erwin Schroedinger said that ever since the Ionians, scientists have depended upon a hypothesis of comprehensibility, a conviction that nature is identical with what can be understood by our minds.

Consequently there was a concealed and insidious humanism in science until Ernst Mach pointed out that the idea of cause and effect is an intrusion of our mind into the domain of nature. The notion of force also projects into the universe, animistically, our own sense of effort or will. Using a new kind of Occam's razor, Mach invoked a principle of economy: we must exclude from our accounts of nature every feature not needed to deal with the observations at hand. Such economy would dispense with a Greek logic that had persisted under plausible terms like *how*, *because, so, in order to, suppose, as a result, although, when,* and so on. Schroedinger, making an effort to limit the vocabulary of science by dropping such terms, calls upon us to speak a language that is not Greek. He agrees with Mach, who wanted science to renounce "image worship." In brief, the scientist has become aware of the gaps in nature, the conditions that are not amenable to logic. He admits that his hypothesis of comprehensibility breaks down at certain places. Scientists themselves have realized that formerly science was another mode of scholasticism.

The scholasticism began when Newton built a fictitious world of bodies obeying a universal mathematical law of gravity. Then the eighteenth century succeeded in setting upon nature a "mathematical finality"—leaving it to the nineteenth century to subject economics, biology, sociology, and even psychology to such mathematical laws, clear as Newtonian logic and inevitable as the classic notion of fate. Nineteenth-century science was thought to be scientific exactly in proportion as it approached the certainty of mathematic. In Bronowski's opinion the laws of cause and effect became so nearly identical with scientific thinking that the Victorians had a compulsion to deal with all their experiences, ethical and psychological as well as scientific, in these categories. Their universe was a machine run by infallible logic—the logic of physics—which turns out to be a way of imposing the mind or the will upon situations that cannot really be known by any such methods. They never paused to ask whether Newton was extending into the universe under the guise of mathematical equations the operations of his own psyche. They never suspected that in Newton's world man was still the center of a natural order conceived by a science that had not yet learned to rely fully on its observations or to exclude our logic from our theories.

By the end of the century it was apparent that chance is no exceptional or secondary effect in nature, but perhaps inherent in nature. Chance, in short, is real; it may be more operative in nature than cause and effect, which are only a large-scale aspect of how things behave. So far as an individual particle goes, behavior is largely random—at least unpredictable. The randomness of separate items manifests itself as cause and effect whenever the activity of numberless particles is cast into statistical measurements. In other words statistical probabilities or possibilities are of greater interest than laws of cause and effect; and probabilities or possibilities arise from chance, not from certainties. In every area of certainty there are margins of uncertainty. The certainty is an abstraction, not an actuality. The randomness is the actuality. In Bronowski's words, the notion of the inevitable has been replaced by degrees of prediction: "Uncertainty *is* the world." The law is a pattern, a trend, a by-effect of large-scale observations; and accordingly the law may not operate in any given instance at any given time. For this reason Bronowski calls the law of cause and effect a scholasticism that in itself has as little to do with scientific method as Aristotle's logic. We must reckon, then, with the reality of what is random, as we did in speaking of the notion of entropy. More disconcerting still, if the random is the real, nature is never given twice to the experimenter in exactly the same state, and inductive logic breaks down: there are happenings that are *not* caused. The motion of each particle in a Brownian movement is haphazard; only the movement of all the particles, or almost all the particles, is a certainty. But the certainty arises from an actuality that is random, and largely inaccessible, to logic. This is absurd: reaction does not follow action.

The exclusion of the scientist's personality from his science has also been required by those who have reinterpreted the laws of force. In older physics, which was to a degree anthropocentric, it was said that objects exerted forces on each other: the force was the cause, and the motion of the objects was the effect. It is now suspected that such laws of force are merely a way of describing how things behave when they exist together in a field. The so-called forces they exert on each other are simply a manifestation of their relation to each other in a certain space. Thus the laws of force are an ambiguous circumlocution. In Musil's phrase, the force exerted by objects on each other is an aspect of the "complex to which they belong." Force has changed from something that seemed positive to something that seems negative, since forces are descriptive, not causative. The forces are not "in" nature but rather are our way of rationalizing what goes on in nature.

In nineteenth-century physics, force was a reality and a cause, as was implied in the magical term "energy," which concealed the humanism in a "dynamic" universe. This magic has been emptied out now that force is thought to be the relationships between things in a space-time field. Our present notion of force has been compared to the middle term of a syllogism that drops out when we reach a conclusion; it is only a means of getting from premise to proof. We now image object A moving thus and so when it appears in a space-time complex created by its relations with objects B, C, and D; and this complex changes—that is, the "forces" exert themselves in other ways—when objects E and F appear in the constellation. In theory it is not necessary to suppose that these bodies are acting on each other by having a mysterious "energy" to attract or repel; instead, any such attraction or repulsion is a characteristic of the space-time complex in which A, B, C, D, and E and F belong. The laws of force, in brief, are a formula for denoting the ways in which things are interdependent as they exist together in areas of space-time that they create about themselves.

This revised view of force dispels one of the grand illusions of the nineteenth century—the belief that nature is dynamic, that the self is will, a mystique that gripped the imagination of philosophers, poets, novelists, as well as scien-

tists. The entire universe was contaminated with an anthropomorphism that was inherent in Newtonian physics,
and had a long history. Aristotle read into nature a Greek
confidence that there is an end toward which all things
strive; and Newton substituted for this entelechy another
sort of projection by reading into astronomy the dynamism
of man's will disguised under a system of gravitational forces.
He tinged classical physics with a romantic psychology (or
a renaissance psychology). The mythology of force took
many forms in the nineteenth century—the form of a "Principle of Development," as Hegel called it, a dialectic by
which the Spirit unfolded itself in the eras of History; or the
form of "evolution," or Carlyle's belief in a World-Urge
(*Welttrieb*) expressing itself in the heroism of great men
or the politics of race. Carlyle put all this faith in dynamics
in one phrase: "Force, Force, everywhere Force; and we
ourselves a mysterious Force in the center of that." The
rebels and supermen of the long romantic twilight were
creatures of an unconditioned will.

Nietzsche, the arch individualist and apostle of total freedom, reduces to absurdity the notion of force on which
Newton's world was conceived. The superman as Nietzsche
conceived him is free; but his freedom is an anarchy of
power. He rides the blast Shelley had loosed in his "Ode to
the West Wind," a tempest that is destroyer as well as
preserver. Whenever Prometheus the liberator is obsessed
by the mystique of force and invokes power to save the
world, he is transformed, as Camus warns, into Prometheus
the tyrant, the megalomaniac. Conrad was among the
moderns who saw what happened when life was made synonymous with a will-to-power; he pondered the disaster of
Kurtz, one who had kicked the world out from under him
to make his will absolute at the heart of darkness. So Marlow
watches Kurtz die whispering the alarming phrase that reveals what he saw when he looked into the abyss of Western
man's will—the horror. Then Eliot picked up the theme

as epigraph for *The Hollow Men*—"Mistah Kurtz, he dead."

To summarize, there was a surprising compatibility between the science and the romanticism of the nineteenth century, since both, in spite of their seeming opposition, sprang from an anthropomorphic view of the world. The romantic frankly created a world as his will or idea. And behind the quasi-dehumanized scientific laws—behind the speciously impersonal mechanics of the physical order—there was a compulsive logic of cause and effect extending man's mind into nature by a theory of force or energy, a reflex of man's own will. That this scheme of forces in a mechanical system was not dehumanized is proved by Hardy's *Jude the Obscure* or *Tess*, novels where the gods play out their malign game with their helpless victims. Tess is destroyed by a machine of fatality that seems to be impersonal, but is actually the working of a logic as tyrannical as the logic of the old Newtonian physics. One never knows what "fate" means in Hardy.

The same tyrannical logic—this time under the guise of social and psychological forces—is in action behind Ibsen's plots, with willful characters going down to defeat before laws that are the fictions of a simplistic science. These plays, like Hardy's novels, have a certain stain of dishonesty, for their neutral laws are not neutral, but the activity of a sort of nemesis never brought into the open or in any way explained or justified or acknowledged. The fatalism in a Hardy novel or an Ibsen drama is humanistic after all—yet assumes none of the larger responsibilities of classical humanism.

In science, in philosophy, in literature—in the mechanistic biology of Huxley, who said there is a clear reason behind every natural law; in the frantic logic of Nietzsche's irrationalism; in Zola's "naturalistic" novels—the anthropomorphic view of the universe deviously affirmed itself to the very end of the last century. The notion of destiny was available to poet and scientist as a means of endorsing the reign of force: in 1900 Ernst Haeckel triumphantly said that the unchanging laws of matter and force made religious myths unnecessary, for God is only a gaseous vertebrate. He called his book *The Riddle of the Universe*, then went on to solve his riddle by proclaiming "the absolute dominion of the great eternal iron laws," and closed his last chapter by quoting Goethe:

> By eternal laws
> Of iron ruled,
> Must all fulfil
> The cycle of
> Their destiny.

The reaction was predictable. It came in science with the theory of relativity and a dozen other theories. It came in painting with cubism and its shifting perspectives. It came in poetry with Eliot and the generation of the First World War. In all three areas it negated romanticism.

From Nietzsche's great blond beast, the entirely free spirit, to Eliot's hollow men: this was the course of affairs up to 1939 and a war that put an end not only to all romanticism but also to every ingrained homocentric view of things. During the twenties and thirties Eliot spoke for those saddened by a depression that closed an era of laissez faire, freedom, and enterprise. Prufrock feels himself lonely and dumb: when he tries to speak, he cannot communicate. He is like Lazarus come from the dead and *to* the dead. He camouflages himself, at teas, on long foggy afternoons, where women come and go. It is said that cubism invented camouflage, and indeed the First World War used camouflage in a cubist way.

Cubism broke up the object into fragmented patterns of changing appearance; eventually it deprived the object of identity entirely. Under the cubist attack the object first disintegrated into uncertain planes, then disappeared into an illusion of the object. The technique of camouflage assumed there was an object to camouflage, that there was a self to take on a protective coloration. Eliot studied this protective coloring in Prufrock and others whispering together quietly and meaninglessly, wearing deliberate disguises; and he assumed that behind all these social compliances and gestures there was really a self, secluded, distracted, timorous, but there somewhere behind the faces one wears. To this extent Eliot's tactic was cubist. Yet just as the new painting has gone beyond cubism, the new a-literature has gone beyond Prufrock.

The organization man is Prufrock's sad descendant. He still supposes he has a self: at least he is trying to heal it, or to find it, as he lies babbling on a couch in offices licensed to practice our new catechisms and confessionals. But the man in the gray flannel suit, though he survives by camouflage, may have little to camouflage. His one care is to fit in; he must fit in to survive. His protective color is a last phase of Darwinian survival by adaptation—an adaptation that is total in an age of total togetherness. The irony is that the nineteenth century thought of survival as a struggle between rugged individuals. This was another romanticism. The rugged individuals forgot that an easier way to survive is to vanish, to avail one's self of an adjustment so total that at last there is nothing to vanish.

Tropisms and Anti-Logic

I

If the organization man is not a very rugged individual, at least he thinks he has his "individual problems" in adjusting. But writers like Nathalie Sarraute and Samuel Beckett have outranged interpersonal psychology. They have examined our adjustments with a finer, more despairing insight; for while we have been trying to adjust, they know that our trouble is more afflicting—we no longer have anything to adjust.

The venture to which Mme. Sarraute has devoted herself is to "touch bottom" in the quicksand of lives given entirely to penny-pinching, gossip, and wary self-protection. Her novels continue the research begun by Sartre in *Nausea*, where Antoine Roquentin tells the Self-Taught Man, "I was just thinking that here we sit, all of us, eating and drinking to preserve our precious existence and really there

is nothing, nothing, absolutely no reason for existing."
Sickened as he is by the inauthenticity of the normal life,
Sartre marvels at ordinary people drinking coffee: "If you
asked them what they did yesterday, they aren't embarrassed." Mme. Sarraute is dejected by the bad faith of
commonplace persons who look innocent enough but who
are not innocent because their existence is a deception.
To judge by their opinions, their actions, their daily trans-
actions, they are as stable as the law of averages; but "underneath, round about, there's nothing: a sheet of white paper."

In 1939 Mme. Sarraute called her disquieting little stories
Tropisms—twenty-four cinematic glimpses of banal situations in everyday Paris. The persons in these situations are
not persons: they *are* simply their reactions to the conditions
they meet; and their reactions are tropistic. There is only
the surface, only the appearance. Their existence has been
equalized by what, in a recent article, Mme. Sarraute calls
the stupefying power of mass communication, which has
made banality a major industry. The women who chat
with each other before a shop window are victims of a
"systematic stultification" and cannot break out of the
cocoon of ready-made notions that are a substitute for
thinking and feeling.

In representing the texture of such lives, Mme. Sarraute
has outdistanced psychology by means of what she calls
"sub-conversation," *sous-conversation*, which is an echo or
a whisper to convey what is wholly expected; so there are
no surprises beyond the shock of recognizing the trite at its
most dismal. These lives are unredeemed. All responses are
quotidian; the drift toward the norm is so constant, nothing
could be said to happen. She goes at things from the outside,
fully alert, and simply listens, like Henry Green, who has
adopted telephone dialogue as a medium for his own novels.
Such telephonic exchange is the discourse of our shabby
routine.

Mme. Sarraute says of her personages "They talk, they

talk, they talk." She taps the surface of commonplace affairs, then waits, hoping the reader can hear the hollow inside. She builds upon Conrad's experiment when Marlow faces the pilgrims on the banks of the Congo and finds them sawdust men; all you have to do, he says, is to stick your finger into them and the sawdust pours out. Mme. Sarraute does not find even sawdust. These figures have only their babble. In fact, Nathalie Sarraute has learned what the nineteenth-century scientist never learned—observation is more revealing than explanation. She is not at pains to account for her findings, but prefers a true phenomenalism, asserting nothing beyond the data. Her art does not try to exceed the limits of the apparent. It is a kind of operationalism in fiction. People are what they do, and these people can survive only in the shallows where everything is obvious.

Thanks to this *ad hoc* scrutiny, her stories are about anti-heroes without the bold features that were so visible, so distinctive, in earlier fiction. All these carefully seen characters are questionable, blurred, for their natures change as they adapt themselves to the others around them. Their presence is a field-effect, giving them a mobile sort of being uncommon in the older novel. Take, for instance, the field-effect as it works in *The Planetarium*, a novel in which nothing much happens while a young man named Alain and his wife Gisèle contrive to displace their Aunt Berthe from her large Paris apartment and move into it themselves. They do oust Aunt Berthe, and during the process we observe that Alain, Gisèle, and Aunt Berthe all are different persons as they come in contact with each other, though they are all mean-minded and fret about whether they should have a chrome handle on the new oak door or whether they should have leather chairs instead of a *bergère*. Some of the chapters retrace the same scene successively, reporting the same conversation from opposite points of view, but with the same depressing results. The novel does not lack a psychology; but the psychology is fluid, discontinuous, truly experimental, proving that the contours of the modern self are tropisms evoked under certain conditions, then disappearing. There is no bottom to these lives. The novel closes with a remark by Germaine Lemaire, a phony intellectual among other phony intellectuals: "Everything in him, everything about him is coming apart . . . I think we're all of us, really, a bit like that." Yet there is nothing to put together, for there is nothing by way of a self behind these figures approaching and evading each other.

It is true that Stendhal's characters had a certain duplicity, Julien Sorel and Fabrizio del Dongo being at odds with themselves like Hamlet. But Julien's conflicts with himself give him a stamp of individuality, however restless and eccentric, whereas Alain Guimiez is always dissolving before our eyes, taken compliantly and continually into the complex of episodes in which he appears. As the adjustable modern man Alain—contemptible, spoiled, whining, sly— is a reflex of the conditions in which he survives. He lacks the authenticity of Stendhal's heroes, who resist in every way they can the pressure of the habitual and who try at every moment to be themselves, baffled though they are by the discords within them.

Claude Mauriac has mentioned how the anti-novel discloses our present human situation without bias. This is a stage of realism the nineteenth century did not touch. Mme. Sarraute reaches a "zero degree" of fiction—and has reached it by a sensitivity of attention that concerns itself only with *appearances*. The aim of the new science is to reach this zero degree of attention, which makes possible a kind of anti-science matching the impartiality of the anti-novel. Neither is disposed to foist a logic, a theory, a system on its data; both are intent on regarding what exists. So the effect of uncertainty heightens as novelist and scientist hesitate to extract explanations from what they have noted at short range.

Mme. Sarraute's persons think and speak nothing but

trivialities, the clichés that are the fabric of their character. She begins where Polonius left off—with the platitude. Polonius lived inauthentically (given to thrift, thrift, Horatio), resting comfortably at the surface of what is conventional. His personality was his chatter, and his chatter was a dread of silence, a camouflage of his suspicion. Polonius was an anti-hero operating by middle-class precautions. However, Shakespeare's drama has another plane of experience, for Hamlet is a counterpoise to Polonius. Or is he? One of the vexing riddles is that *both* Polonius and Hamlet speak platitudes; but we are never sure whether Hamlet's banalities are really banalities or prophetic insights into the human condition. Conversely, when Hamlet quarters his thoughts, the banalities spoken by Polonius look, by contrast with Hamlet's subtleties, like common sense. Hamlet's monologue on the question of being or not being is a shocking parallel to the banality of Polonius' advice to Laertes: "To thine own self be true." Polonius babbles; and Hamlet's speculation about conscience making cowards of us all, about finding quarrel in a straw when honor's at stake, is another sort of babble? Hamlet's ponderings can be read as thoughts for this week: they are shocking exactly because we are aware that Hamlet ought not to be speaking platitudes— or else they are not platitudes but discoveries? In any case the play exploits platitudes; but all the platitudes are ambiguous since they seem to mean something acute when they are in Hamlet's mouth, although he actually *says* what, in another tone, Polonius might say.

The ambiguity is gone in Mme. Sarraute's novels: all the platitudes are spoken by Polonius. There is no counterpoint—only the anti-hero. *The Planetarium* reports accurately the insipid, anonymous, stale quality of our existence as it is described by Heidegger, who accuses us of taking a plunge into the quotidian. Heidegger sees this as a second fall of man, from authenticity into everyday concerns that absorb us in situations which are not ours. This state of

Verfallen—the descent to prattle—is, in Heidegger's opinion, a result of our overinvolvement in the moment, our petty worries about getting on, a loss of any view of the far horizon of our being, the future that is death or nothingness. Nobody has more dismally shown our submissiveness to the others, to sordid desires and anxieties, than Mme. Sarraute.

In L'Ere du Soupçon she says that the new novel has lost interest in the immobile solid hero of the past, and attends, instead, to one who has decomposed into the drifting sentiments she calls inconnues. Her characters have changing features as when light plays over things, and her hero is a shadow of himself. He is anonymous, like K or HCE or the nameless "I," though he rouses our mistrust (méfiance). She rejects all "dangerous resemblance" and relies on the cliché, which catches us off guard. In a monotone she records the Bavard—the Bromide—a language more insidious and revealing than the sharply accented dialogue of the theater, on which the nineteenth-century novel relied. By such delicacy she hopes to get beyond the old psychology and to detect mouvements infimes, the small changes in language and feeling that are at once exterior and interior. Her people wear the "carapace of the ordinary"; the essence of their nature is their scheming. The treachery of their existence—for their self is only a shadow—appears in a psychology of small talk about buying a house, a transaction suggesting that Martereau is both reliable and dishonest.

One of the most significant titles in the modern novel is Portrait of a Man Unknown. A double meaning attaches to the phrase, for the anonymous narrator tries to "touch bottom" in his own life and in the lives of a stingy old man who distrusts his daughter, a girl in ill health who is interested in getting herself engaged to a fellow with enough money to remodel the house where they will live. In a museum the narrator sees a Portrait of a Man Unknown by some anonymous Dutch painter. The anonymity of the work is pleasing and comforting: "there's something uplifting" about it. Being anonymously painted and representing an anonymous figure, the portrait seems to be a screen behind which there is some security for the self, which has withdrawn itself, erased itself, as far as it can. For this reason, too, the figure of a man unknown, impersonal as it is, seems to be honest, as actual people do not seem to be. The "uncertain outlines" of the one painted figure suggest that we all exist by a sort of absence. The Portrait of a Man Unknown enables us to endure the normal, the average, the doubtful. But in our everyday affairs nothing is more diseased than the normal. This is what gave Sartre nausea.

Both Sartre and Mme. Sarraute are referring to the mystery of the ordinary, especially in its banal forms. This sense of the mystery—possibly the sinister quality—in what is common was precisely what was lacking in nineteenth-century realism. We are now vulnerable to the usual—perhaps we have been ever since Kafka startled us by his over-response to what seems normal and customary. Our most acute anxieties are aroused by what the nineteenth century took to be natural. For us, nothing is more suspicious than the obvious. The realistic novel of the nineteenth century was filled with banalities painstakingly described. But the foundations of this realism were solid, public, and based upon scientific laws operating with a known logic. There was nothing untrustworthy about the commonplace: it was simply dull. The realists like Balzac and Gautier had confidence in the existence of their world ("For me the world is *there*") just as they had confidence in the existence of their humdrum characters. The very stupidities in Balzac were a desperate attempt to embed the novel in actualities that could not be questioned—any more than the substance of matter could be questioned. Père Goriot had his eighteen shirts of fine linen "the delicate texture of which was rendered more conspicuous by the two pins set with large diamonds, and connected with a little chain . . . He usually wore a light blue coat, and put on daily a fresh white piqué waistcoat, under which his round protuberant stomach rose and fell, swinging his heavy gold chain and trinkets attached to it." Père Goriot undeniably exists in a world of real things as demonstrable and established as the solar system or the cash value of some thriving business. Balzac obviously convinced himself, first of all, that Goriot is there.

It was characteristic of this naïve, unsuspicious realism that it should resort to an arbitrary logic of melodrama, of either/or choices so mutually exclusive that plots were mechanisms where even chance was rationalized into a carefully fabricated structure of events leading to a "conclusion." Père Goriot dies while his daughters dance. This melodramatic climax could happen only in a world where there was a falsely dramatic logic, where events were decisive, like the forces working in the physical order. Most of the tragic effects in this solid world of realistic fiction took the form of a melodramatic fate as final and imperious as the eternal iron laws of nature.

II

Far from being tragic, the shadowy characters in Mme. Sarraute's novels seem negligibly trivial, if not comic. If the essence of comedy be incongruity, then the comic, not the tragic, is at the center of our experience. This is why Eugène Ionesco has importance: he writes nonsense, his plays being made of prattle, his anti-theater being a kind of behaviorism reduced to absurdity. Ionesco deals with the tropism more whimsically, more philosophically, than Mme. Sarraute. Why the conventional theater bores him Ionesco has explained several times. Even Pirandello is, for him, passé, and our psychological dramas are inadequately psy-

chological. Ionesco wishes to give up all the tricks—the
ficelles—that make our stage phony, and to press his theater
beyond the safety zone, as he calls it. He wants to endorse
the *insoutenable* by upsetting all remaining conventions.
One way of doing this is to present the quotidian, the
automatic behavior that conceals—and also reveals—the
strangeness and the bathos of our lives. Thus all his plays
are comedies, or, as he prefers to call them, tragical farces,
where he tries to be as contemporary as the new painting.
One can deal with modern man only by derision, since the
behavior of man in his world is nonsensical, not tragic.
Because comedy has an instinct for what is absurd, it is
more desperate than tragedy, discounting both hope and
despair as tragedy cannot.

Like Heidegger, Ionesco is fascinated by the gulf of
nothingness, the "emptiness," that underlies our existence.
In one of his interviews he says that he cannot take life
seriously because its horrors are incredible: "I really have
the feeling that life is nightmarish, that it is painful, un-
endurable as a bad dream. Just glance around you: wars,
catastrophes and disasters, hatreds and persecutions, death
awaiting us on every side." This is the feeling that penetrates
Beckett's contemporary comedy. Kafka dreamed these things
before they were actualities; but now that we have witnessed
them, they seem more than ever like a dream. "Nay," Hamlet protested, "I know not seems. It is." Ionesco and Beckett
reverse this statement: "Nay, I know not is. It seems." In
other words, it cannot be. This is also the theme of dramas
by Jean Genet, who takes living to be an illusion.

Is it coincidental that Ionesco should use the same phrases
as Mme. Sarraute? He says, for example, that his anti-theater
(exactly like Mme. Sarraute's anti-novels) puts the absurd
within our grasp by means of "our everyday conversation."
He tells us that his point of departure is his discovery that
language has fallen to pieces, that our words are noises
without sense, proving we are automatons living in a useless

world above which the sky is a façade for nothingness. His characters have no identity; they easily become the opposites of themselves. Thus "nothing seems more surprising than the banal." All Ionesco has to do, he believes, is to listen, without trying to urge upon us any syllogisms. He feels a certain euphoria in making these discoveries, since "to feel the absurdity of the commonplace, and of language—its falseness—is already to have gone beyond it." This euphoria gives his theater an air of the comic we miss in Nathalie Sarraute's novels; but then again, the comic in Ionesco goes to show how we are in a tragic condition. The contemporary writer must of necessity present the significance of what is utterly habitual.

Since he refuses to be "serious," Ionesco has given up the game of politics. One of his essays for the press is titled "My Plays Don't Try to Save the World." Unlike the existentialists, he will not use his pen to commit himself to causes, programs, policies. He is not engaged. Instead, he believes a drama should have no conscious intention to teach anything whatever: "I detest a reasoning play." As Ionesco sees it, the difference between theater and anti-theater is precisely here, since anti-theater "liberates" us, he says, from all programs. However, he does seem to agree with the statement made by one of his characters in *The Killer*—The Man who remarks, "Science and art have done far more than politics to change our attitudes. The true revolution has occurred in scientific laboratories, in artists' studios. Einstein, Oppenheimer, Breton, Kandinsky, Picasso, Pavlov—there are the genuine innovators. They widen the field of our awareness, review our vision of the world, change us." Ionesco seems to know that our science has affected the nature of our literature, making all verbal language a cliché, and a rather crude cliché at that, considering the statements it is possible to phrase in the idiom of higher mathematics.

Apropos of this recent breakdown in language, George Steiner has claimed that until the end of the seventeenth century language had a capacity to refer to reality and to represent experience by words. But the new mathematics, like abstract painting or the new music, cannot be verbalized. Mathematics has so deeply invaded all the sciences, as well as philosophy, that language no longer serves to express the range of reality when the world we live in is like a game played by topologists, whose mathematic is able to erect structures so far beyond the boundaries of the old logic that they cannot be described in any vocabulary except a nonverbal one.

Ionesco wrote his first drama in 1948, *The Bald Soprano*, as a tragedy of language, using the stereotyped dialogues he found in the Assimil-method primer from which he was learning English. As he studied the clichés in this exercise book—"there are seven days in the week, it costs too much, I don't have the right change, the room is too warm, where is the W. C."—he felt the text changing under his eyes: it began to ferment, he says, and he saw that these automatic colloquies represented very well the collapse of our daily lives. We go on speaking as if we were stricken by some sort of amnesia. So Ionesco wrote his anti-play in which the Smiths and the Martins talk, talk, talk the babble that sounds, when one is able really to hear it, appallingly like what one hears at any cocktail party. The characters disintegrate into the jargon that serves us as a way of life

Mr. Smith: One must always think of everything.
Mrs. Martin: The ceiling is above, the floor is below.
Mrs. Smith: When I say yes, it is only a manner of speaking.
Mrs. Martin: To each his own.

This may sound like Dada after the First World War. It is not, for there is a tenable psychology underneath Ionesco's plays, and like Nathalie Sarraute or Samuel Beckett, he is coping with the anonymity inherent in the modern self. Words, actions have become an empty shell, which is what he means by a collapse of reality. Consider, for example, the verbalism of existence in a day when a Nazi who has admittedly been responsible for killing some millions of persons is brought to trial by carefully arranged legal protocol so that his guilt may be demonstrated. Our intoxication with verbal nonsense has also been studied by Raymond Queneau, whose *Exercices de Style* inspired Ionesco. In these exercises Queneau ninety-nine times treats the episode of a ride on a bus, each time using a different idiom.

The absurdities in Ionesco are not merely verbal, for he is often Kafkaesque. In *The New Tenant* a man rents a room that entirely disappears behind the furniture he moves into it—furniture that obliterates not only the apartment but the street outside and finally the whole world. *The Future Is In Eggs* is Ionesco's biting satire on overpopulation. A young couple are told by their relatives to produce, for the good of posterity—Produce something, be a man. So Roberta lays an egg; and Jacques does too. The parents come in with the eggs: "They're my daughter's very first eggs; they look just like her." And what are we going to make with these offspring? Omelettes. Sausage meat. Humanitarians. Anti-humanitarians. Radishes. Radicals. Chemists. Firemen. Teachers. Existentialists. Brothers and half-brothers. And omelettes, above all, omelettes. "Long live production. Long live the white race. As it was in the past, the future lies in eggs."

Ionesco wants the unfamiliar to erupt amid the familiar, and his theater is best explained by one of his own characters, the poet Nicolas in *Victims of Duty*. We must, says Nicolas, use a new logic and a new psychology based on antagonism and contradiction: "I should introduce contradiction where there is no contradiction, and no contradiction where there is what common-sense usually calls contradiction. . . . We'll get rid of the principle of identity and unity of character and let movement and dynamic psychology take its place. We are not ourselves. Personality doesn't exist. . . . Each character is not so much himself as another. . . . As for plot and motivation, let's not mention them. We ought to ignore them completely, at least in their old form, which was too clumsy, too obvious, too phoney, like anything that's too obvious."

In other words, Ionesco discards the laws of cause and effect on which both theater and science had been built. Instead he accepts a system of logic to which Nicolas refers, the logic of Stéphane Lupasco, whose work gives us the key to what Ionesco is doing in theater. In his little-known book *Logic and Contradiction* (1947) Lupasco summarizes the ideas by which he is attempting to make a huge revision of Western methods of reasoning, and he relies upon an existential dialectic that he calls a logic of antagonism. "Logic," he states, "must become the basic science of the dynamic contraries in human experience." His main point is that the old logic, derived from Aristotle, was static, not dynamic, because it started from a principle of noncontradiction: that is, anything was true if it was not contradictory. Conversely, anything contradictory could not be true. Hence conventional logic ruled out the illogical as unreal, sterilizing its ability to deal with existence, which is filled with antagonisms, contradictions, and illogicalities. Lupasco calls the old logic bipolar, since it was able to assign only two values to everything—true and false. This was like the old ethic based upon good and bad, or the old esthetic based upon the beautiful and the ugly. The test of truth has always been its consistency: to be contradictory was to be false; so the contradictory did not exist. Falsity did not exist. But falsity does exist.

If falsity does not exist, evil does not exist, folly does not exist; nor, I presume, does comedy exist. If logic cannot accommodate cross-purposes, antagonisms, uncertainties, inconsistencies, double premises, it has no relevance to life. From the Greeks onward, logic was able to work with only the true; and if nothing is true but the true, then truth is a mere tautology. Under this closed system, an accident was not amenable to the methods of logic. What could not be explained by a sequence of logical steps was simply an error in observation or experiment, a chance that could safely be ruled out. Consequently science was a system of invariables, constants, and necessities that denied, excluded, or ignored the inexplicable in our most immediate experience. Then too, the older logic excluded the feelings; but the feelings are an envelope for logic and for what we experience. Furthermore, feelings are unique—since no feeling is exactly like another feeling; thus our feelings are discontinuous, occurring without any logical sequence. Worse still, feelings evade thought, so they cannot be rationalized. In brief, the old logic was a means of excluding or narrowing experience, not a means of dealing with experience. Under past systems of logic one could know clearly; but the more clearly one knew, the more one ignored; thus the less one knew.

It can be noted in passing that if what Lupasco says is valid, then tragedy has always had the ability logic lacked in dealing with the absurdity of life. Tragedy, we say, has its own dialectic, for it deals with the contraries in human experience. The double vision of tragedy gives rise to irony. But then again, irony was not amenable to the old logic. In his own way Lupasco is taking seriously many of the things we have always said about the tragic view of life; he is taking them seriously enough to try to enrich logic with the tragic understanding of human experience, which is, of course, an existential way of treating human experience. Lupasco is emphasizing that logic has not been truly dialectical—not even the Marxist logic, which has also labored under a delusion that it could finally master the contraries in history, and put an end to them. We must remember, also, that there is a comic dialectic as well as a tragic dialectic, since comedy has its own interest in the absurdity of man.

III

The trouble with the old logic, then, was that it did not admit the reality of the false; to presume that nothing is true but the true is one means of walking out of reality into the security of a system. Lately Percy Bridgman has made the same point in his book *The Way Things Are*, where he notes that it is nonsense to say that statement A has no meaning; for it has a sort of meaning. What is the meaning of a meaningless statement? Bridgman takes logic to be a way of projecting into the future certain kinds of regularity we have found in past experience; it is in us, perhaps, rather than in things. Individual events never recur; but our scientific account of events is a generalization based upon certain recurrences, ruling out differences that we say make no difference. How, furthermore, can we verify a statement that the sun rose yesterday? Bridgman brings the skepticism of David Hume into modern science, and thus approves of an operationalism that is a kind of existential logic: Science is only what scientists *do* when they perform experiments; but since no experiment really can be repeated, any laws based upon experiments are logical artifacts. Bridgman is trying to make science accommodate itself more nearly to the actual scientific experience; he is trying to draw science back from theory to observation.

Therefore Bridgman, like Lupasco, accepts the principle of antagonism and contradiction, and the actuality of what was false according to the old logic of scientific law.* Both are using a new anti-logic. This anti-logic reappears in another form in what is called metamathematics, by which Kurt Goedel re-examines the premises of mathematic just as Lupasco re-examines Aristotelian logic. In Goedel's opinion it is impossible to prove that any logical system does not contain contradictions inherent in the theorems derived

* See Appendix, "Note on *Decision, Order, and Time in Human Affairs*, by G. L. S. Shackle."

from the system. To prove a system correct, one must get outside the system. To do so is difficult, if not impossible, since mathematics cannot get outside mathematics—at least by mathematical methods. Goedel finds that mathematical systems have severe limits, since each system is based either on inconsistencies or on tautologies: "No matter how much we extend our mathematics, there will always remain certain valid propositions whose validity cannot be decided within the framework of mathematics." He is forced to admit that some mathematical statements fall into an area of uncertainty he calls undecidable; they cannot be proved or disproved, and they may contain unresolvable contradictions within themselves.

A Goedelian paradox is illustrated by the statement: "The statement made in this statement is false." This statement can be true only if it is false. Here is a situation in mathematics like the old philosophic crux used by Jean-Paul Sartre to describe the illusions and mirror-effects in Genet's plays: "Epimenides says that Cretans are liars. But Epimenides is a Cretan. Therefore Cretans are not liars." Or it is like the map of a city in which the map itself is located, which must show the map within the city. In any case Goedel takes formal mathematical systems to be incomplete and self-limited because there are valid propositions inaccessible to proof within the framework of mathematics. By indicating the limits of mathematical consistency and by emphasizing the contradiction and paradox in mathematical logic, Goedel brings about a "crisis in the foundations" of theory, as Georg Cantor did before him with his theory of infinite sets. In the same spirit Ionesco has pressed theatrical logic to its limits, and painters like Jean Dubuffet have pressed painting to its limits—or beyond, perhaps.

In still other ways science is faced with a breakdown in the logic of cause and effect, for this illogicality in mathematic is supported by evidence of illogical behavior in the atom and light. According to the quantum theory, energy is emitted in certain units, or at certain levels, and there seems to be no way of predicting accurately which units will be emitted in any one instance at any given time. Particles behave with a logic of discontinuity. And light behaves both like waves and particles. To complicate matters, we can locate the position of a particle at any instant, or we can determine its speed; but we cannot do both at the same time, apparently because in measuring very small quantities the observer by his very observing somehow gets between what is being measured and the measurement he makes. Thus there is always a margin of uncertainty—the uncer-certainty principle, as Heisenberg calls it, which is a sign of the irreducible inaccuracy of our knowledge. Heisenberg puts it this way: the logic of classical physics has broken down simply because any measuring device constructed by classical physics belongs to the world described by classical physics and therefore introduces uncertainties into any measurements needed to describe the activity of very small quantities that seemingly do not obey the laws of classical physics. Our knowledge is equivocal or illogical because we cannot get outside our own measuring system.

As a result we are forced to explain our observations by the concepts of classical physics even while we know these concepts do not fully apply to the world of atomic activity. I take it that Heisenberg is underscoring what Goedel and Bridgman have said: that only by accepting the inconsisten-cies and contradictions in reality can we get outside the boundaries of our old naïve logic. Classic logic does not apply systematically to the experience of modern man, to his observation or knowledge. Therefore the only way we can deal with these contradictory but actual situations is by Niels Bohr's principle of complementarity, accepting as true *both* terms of a contradiction. We get further by assuming that light is both particles and waves than by insisting it must be either, as classical physics would have done. One limitation of nineteenth-century science was that it preferred a logic of causality even if some of the observations it made did not fit this logic. Thus an unwarranted coherence and necessity were thrust upon experience. Scientists today usually presume that a logic of causality makes available consistent laws that are to be used as tools of science rather than as a description of reality. Consistency is sought, but hardly expected. So scientists are willing to tolerate a logic of contradiction—an anti-logic—in order to come to terms with the facts they observe.

Lupasco calls his logic a discontinuous quanta-formation, and he accepts as usable the affirmative, the negative, and all the values that appear between these poles regardless of their consistency. The old logic of *sic et non* succumbs to a logic drawn from experience, where contraries, illogically, coexist. Such is the trend in Wittgenstein and the Vienna group, which admits what Whitehead said very simply: contradictions are inherent in reality. Any system that brings total consistency into reality is probably specious. Here was the block in past philosophies: they sacrificed truth for consistency; they were imperialist because they tried to subdue the universe to the categories of the mind. Since the old logic ruled out the false, it froze truth into certainties; it detoured around variables, deviations, and chance—all of which seemed signs of error. In reaction, Lupasco seeks an existential logic, a logic that is filled with "creative contradictions" and looks upon the absolute as a menace. If logic is to be existential, it must embrace our emotional along with our rational experience; it must involve error as well as truth, the discordant as well as the harmonious. And the new science deals with accident, chance, the special case, as well as with the necessary. The single exception is as real as the "law." The negative is as real as the positive. Antimatter seems to exist as well as matter. Meanwhile Samuel Beckett is saying that nothing is more real than nothing.

Lupasco invokes a logic of absurdity, a logic that has something in common with the koan exercise in Zen Buddhism. The purpose of a koan exercise is to jar the mind loose from a purely intellectual reading of experience, which is a mere abstraction, and to make us receptive to what is concrete, what is actual, what is inexplicable by reason. Zen assumes that the mind is a trap in which we catch ourselves. Anything that can be rationally stated is an assertion of the surface mind, an effort to dominate the world by reason. In interpreting Zen, Erich Fromm has remarked that in order to cope with the reality of our experiences we need a logic of paradox, accepting a principle that A and not-A do not exclude each other. The Marxist dialectic, of course, stressed the unity of opposites; yet compared with the flexibility of the existential dialectic, which is directed at the single case or the exception, even the Marxist dialectic is too schematic and over-rationalized, addressed not to understanding but commanding the world. The psychoanalyst, the scientist, the artist tell us that cerebration gives a false sense of being in touch with the world. By an extreme reaction, Zen seeks an immediate grasp of reality without any intellectual contamination.

Something of this new instinct for immediacy has gone into Ionesco's plays, with their psychology of antagonism and contradiction, an uncertainty psychology fatal to the logic of plot, motivation, and action, and to the bipolar values of tragic and comic, the prefabricated character, the solved problem. Again we recall how Shakespeare relied upon an uncertainty-principle in writing *Hamlet*, which has a psychology of contradiction, a confusion of tragic with comic, and even a sense of the phoniness (the *ficelles*) of conventional theater, offering us nothing but dumb shows and noise. In speaking to the players, Hamlet anticipates the methods of Ionesco's anti-theater, which is a continual improvising, a constant reversal toward the unexpected. Just as *Hamlet* uses a play within a play, Ionesco's *Improvisation* is built of repetitions that make this drama a mirror-image more suggestive and more elusive than the mirror-images in Pirandello. At the start, Ionesco is writing a play when Bartholomeus I enters, asks him about his play, which he starts to describe; then Bartholomeus II enters, asks him what he is doing, and he starts again to describe his play; then Bartholomeus III enters, asks what he is doing . . . and so on. (Whitehead had the notion that reality is the recurrence of certain appearances.) The three figures of Bartholomeus lecture Ionesco on the technique of the theater, and they start to enact Ionesco's play, putting up signs here and there: Fake Chair, False Table, Phoney Place. They tell Ionesco he's made the blunder of being himself: "Be Ionesco without being Ionesco." This is a little like Goedel's examination of the context of mathematics, and it ends with the same conclusion that any formal system sooner or later reaches the limits of its logic. We must at all costs get outside the system. Ionesco does this by leaping beyond *les ficelles*, by fixing attention on the fakes the stage offers us. Or, as Hamlet urged: "Leave thy damnable faces, and begin."

IV

There is also a connection between Ionesco's anti-theater and the critique of science made as early as 1927 by Percy Bridgman in *The Logic of Modern Physics*, proposing an approach to scientific problems by operationalism. Bridgman fell back upon this operationalism after the classical concepts of physics proved inadequate to deal with the seemingly illogical situations Einstein and others had met in developing the theory of relativity. Admitting the deficiency in classical notions, Bridgman argued that what goes on in nature cannot be put into any formula; therefore we need to get the scientist back to a pure empiricism, to fix his attention on what he observes. He held that a concept in physics is really nothing more than the operations a physicist goes through: "The concept is synonymous with the corresponding set of operations." What we should think is only what we can *do*. Take, for example, the notion of "length," which turns out to be only the operations one goes through in applying a metrical scale to an object; but in every measurement there is a spectrum of uncertainty on account of the constantly changing conditions under which measurements are made. The length *is* only the operation we perform in measuring. Besides, the operations we go through in making a metrical measurement are quite different from the operations we go through in reckoning astronomical distances or the speed of light; consequently there is a difference between a tactile concept of length and an optical concept of length, since two dissimilar operations, under quite different experimental conditions, have been followed in defining "length." Optical length is not the same as tactual length. The result of such discrepancies is that every concept must be used only as an account of what we do in arriving at the concept. Needless to add, this attitude demands a "far-reaching change in all our habits of thought" so that there will be a correspondence between our experience and our ideas, between what we do and what we say or think; and there will always be around every concept a margin of imprecision.

In effect, Ionesco's anti-theater brings operationalism into full use. A play is what happens when a play is acted. This operationalism began in theater with Pirandello, whose plays were "comedies in the making." It continues in anti-painting by Dubuffet, Pollock, or any of the "action" painters, whose painting is what happens when the painter goes through the operation of painting: so execution precedes design—or, if you will, any design is identical with its execution. In this painting, it is often said, painting precedes thinking.

This operationalism—which amounts to a distrust of logic—is everywhere in the anti-drama now being written: not only in Jack Gelber's *The Connection,* a piece that is improvised as it goes, but, more notably, in pieces by Jean

Genet with their dazzling "whirligigs between appearance and reality," as Sartre calls them. *Les Nègres* is "a play for an all-black cast." But, Genet asks, "What exactly is a black? First of all, what's his color?" In *The Maids* he disclaims all certainties by an "absolute state of artifice" where each character plays the role of a character playing a role. The shifting of roles, with changes from appearance into being and back again into appearance, is the structure of the drama in *The Balcony*. The contradictions are heightened by having the female roles played by men. In *The Maids*, Claire, who is merely *acting* the role of Madam, whom she plans to murder, is herself murdered by her own suicidal and willful playing of her role. Claire is playing the role of a servant who is playing a role, in which role she is overtaken by actuality, by herself. As Sartre says, Genet's plays, like his novels, are discontinuous actions where non-being is penetrated by being, being by non-being. The drama is the operations performed on the stage: this is its entire "meaning."

Samuel Beckett is more concerned with the artifice of personality than with the artifice of theater. The anti-drama *Endgame* uses the same sort of dialogue we hear in Ionesco's *Bald Soprano*—the cliché that is not a cliché, nonsense that is not nonsense. Hamm asks whether "we are not beginning to mean something." Clov replies: "Mean something! You and I mean something! Ah, that's a good one." Or Vladimir says while waiting for Godot, "We're in no danger of ever thinking any more." And Lucky, when asked to reason a little, says "Quaquaquaqua."

I have called the anti-logic in anti-literature or anti-science existential; but in many ways it might be called post-existential because a dissolution of the self is involved—as we suspect in Gelber and Genet, not to mention Beckett. A preceding generation of writers like Gide tried to assassinate the conventional hero in characters like Lafcadio, Protos, and Amédée Fleurissoire. Gide assassinated the novel itself in *The Counterfeiters*, while cubist painters were assassinating the object. In 1937 Gide wrote "Some Reflections on the Abandoning of Subject in the Plastic Arts." It was printed while abstract painting was demolishing the object so completely that nonobjective art appeared.

We know what happened to the object at the hands of post-cubist painters, who completed the dismantling started by the cubist camouflage; and what happened to the old logic of representation in "action" painters like Pollock, De Kooning, Hartung, and the Paris group with Mathieu, Soulages, and those who have rejected the world to get beyond things. In this range of painting there may have been an original motif—even Kandinsky seems to have started with a thing, which then became a feeling, a rhythm, an explosion of color. Often the painter, as Picasso said, started with something, then destroyed it. During the destruction the thing dispersed into a field-representation, a passage excerpted from process—which is nature seen in its submicroscopic activity. Only at some distance does nature present formal designs. At closer quarters the logic of process is obscure, if not unreadable.

The Zero Degree of Painting

I

Speaking of his anti-plays, Ionesco says that he wants to reach beyond his own day as the painter does, "pressing beyond the safety zone." It is hardly by chance that Jean Dubuffet says of his anti-paintings "I very much like things to be carried to their extreme possible limit. I like painting at the limit of no longer being a painting." If Ionesco is bored by the conventional theater, Dubuffet has exclaimed: "A bas les galeries! A bas les musées! A bas les marchands de tableaux et les critiques d'art!" Dubuffet's purpose is to "evade the painting" just as Ionesco's is to evade the theater, or Beckett's purpose, or Robbe-Grillet's, is to evade the novel. What painters like Dubuffet and Fautrier have particularly refused is the nineteenth-century "touch," the signature of the individual temperament. In fact Dubuffet has called his most-discussed works *Assemblages*, for they are passages "cut out" and thrown together into a "texturology" that seems to erase entirely the personality of the painter. He likes to think of his painting as a stretch of pigment featureless as a gravel walk. Above all he wants to exclude the anecdote. These texturologies have been called formless; but, as Robbe-Grillet has pointed out about his novels, "A new form always seems to be more or less an absence of any form at all, since it is unconsciously judged by reference to consecrated forms."

Robbe-Grillet and the new novelists are known as *chosistes* since they also, with the anti-painters, are working toward the disappearance of the artist in his work, which levels man with things. Until the rise of cubism, Jean Grenier remarks, man was a prisoner of his own image. Western painting was anthropocentric. Then with the cubist analysis of the object, the *nature morte*, instead of man, became the center of art. This was already true of Picasso's painting. Gertrude Stein once told Picasso she had at last found a name for his painting of Three Musicians: "It's a still life." When the cubists got inside the geometry of the object, man lost his primacy in the world of painting, gradually disappearing from the images he made. Ortega y Gasset looked upon this disappearance with foreboding, fearful lest art be dehumanized. It was—rapidly. Nature was absorbing the one who contemplated it. The painter was among the first to sense that man was about to be deposed. Somewhat before the *chosiste* novelist the painter saw that "Things are things, and man is only man." (The phrase is Robbe-Grillet's.)

Until the close of the nineteenth century, painting—impressionism, symbolism, expressionism—had been anthropocentric. To be sure, the impressionists bathed their scenes in an atmosphere, but often this atmosphere was not nature's climate so much as a "harmony" of mood. The impressionists had a highly personal vision. After cubism (Michel Tapié thinks the change came between 1910 and 1920) man appeared in another perspective—not man against nature, or nature seen through an eye, but man as an aspect of things. Soon, under the influence of a new science, things themselves became only a system of relationships, and nature itself disappeared amid atomic activities that are statistical probabilities rather than actualities.

Nature having thus been vacated, the arts were all attempts to subtract. The object tends to vanish from painting; the cubists found that black—an absence of color—has positive value; and in order to formalize the negative or the absent, painters like Lucio Fontana deliberately set about creating nothing by punching holes in their compositions, while Henry Moore made space negative by perforating his sculptures. This method of anti-statement is also found in the novel, for Gide tried to "strip" his fiction of all that is not "pure" by subtracting everything photography or the phonograph could register. In drama Beckett experiments with a decrement in character by having Krapp listen to the tapes he once recorded—an act of minus composition in the theater, subtracting dialogue. After these subtractions are made, the figure of man is a supernumerary, withdrawing as far as it can.

Jean Grenier has set the main question: in spite of all this dehumanizing, all this anti-romanticism, does there remain a certain kind of humanism? A humanism that is not anthropocentric? Have we not, since the Greeks, confused humanism with anthropomorphism? Is it thinkable that anti-painting, like anti-literature, is humanistic in a form we have not yet recognized? Any such humanism would be selfless in a way classic humanism was not; for classic humanism—and romantic humanism—put man at the center, whereas this more self-obliterating humanism would bring man into a less egocentric relation with things. It would in any event be a humanism hard for Western man to accept, requiring a humility we have often praised but seldom practiced.

Without making any great claims for anti-painting and anti-literature as "art," can we consider them as symptomatic of a new relation between man and the universe into which he has been thrown? Perhaps this relation is implied in the strange loss of painting in Dubuffet, whose *Assemblages* are apparently only a random texture of pigment. They are called *Assemblages* because they are in part a result of chance rather than a composition. Dubuffet sets out to get back to zero, to create works where pattern has no part. In 1948 he said, "I think of paintings that would be uniformly made of a single monochrome mud without any variation in colors, or of values, or even of relief of textures, and which would bring out only all those kinds of marks, traces, and live imprints of a hand working the pigment."

Quite literally this painting is operationalism in art, for the composition is entirely what the hand of the painter does in working; it annihilates the motif, or makes the motif, the "idea," what the motion of the painter's hand is, not what the painter "says." Nor is this formlessness inert, since it has the texture of process, a "going on in the universe," of which man's nature is one aspect—possibly an accidental aspect. Dubuffet holds the human and the natural in the same perspective, and he has an "organic sensibility" of a more thoroughgoing kind than Words-worth, who said over a century ago that man and nature are essentially adapted to each other. The operationalism in Dubuffet's painting is muscular—his painting is what his muscles do; and his muscles are an organic phase of the activity proceeding in a universe where things closest to us are problematic. In responding to the natural, Dubuffet turns to the ordinary: "I cannot help feeling that the things closest to us, the most constantly before our eyes, are also the ones that have at all times been the least perceived, that they remain the least known." The statement might have been made by Wordsworth; and it might be made also by Robbe-Grillet or any of the *chosiste* writers who, like

113

Nathalie Sarraute, are perplexed by usual things. Since the painter's muscular activity is a phase of cosmic process, what seems to be random and accidental is actually a facet of necessity: accident is necessity. In this long perspective, the random is fated.

Michel Tapié is the theorist of the "brutal" or "informal" art of Dubuffet or Fautrier. He likes to call it simply *un art autre*. It is *autre* because it is a total revolt against classicism in every form, and is unlike anything the West has seen. Tapié links this *autre* painting with recent science insofar as it accepts the unclassical principle of contradiction, and especially because it uses what he terms *la logistique ensembliste*. This logic traces back to a mathematician, Évariste Galois, who about 1830 worked out a "theory of groups," later extended by Georg Cantor into a theory of infinite sets. Tapié believes that painters like Damian, Sam Francis, and Capogrossi, who take a single element and multiply it indefinitely into a monochromatic expanse, are using a *structure ensembliste* illustrating the principle of continuity in science. To Tapié's satisfaction "informal" painting discards classical structures and motifs in favor of an *échelle des ensembles*, a scale of aggregates that extends the composition far beyond "all the zones commonly called normal." The new art is transfinite. Thus the slightly varied repetitions in Ionesco's plays are a kind of theatrical *structure ensembliste*.

In 1953 Tapié thought it "inevitable we should have an art worthy of the uncertainty principle, the logic of the contradictory, the unlimited rhythms based upon the most complicated concepts of number, of forms reconstituted according to the continuity of the topologies of wholes . . ." He is convinced that *autre* painting moves from the measurable to the infinite, from all past harmonies to a "contradictory universe wherein are juxtaposed the quantitative discontinuous and the qualitatively continuous." Today's "brutal" painter welcomes the accidental as being the spontaneous—as well as being the necessary. Dubuffet has frankly and humorously said of his own spontaneously achieved work, "I'm always on the brink of the foulest and most wretched daubing—and of the small miracle."

Another spontaneous painter venturing to daub—miraculously—is Jean Fautrier, who also uses *structures ensemblistes* and works in series. He too is an operationalist in painting, relying on what his hand executes, not upon a motif. He spatters, sprays, smears pigments; or pastes up his surfaces. About 1930 Fautrier gave up painting on canvas because it sucks up pigment and thus obscures the action of the hand; he resorted to smearings on paper, later doused with varnish to fix the texture. His work has been compared to pastry. Gradually he was led to treat "objects" in series—boxes, folded paper, dominoes, bobbins, dice, tubes—because he finds these things esoteric in their own right, and also because using these everyday things prevents him from using his own "touch." Fautrier ridicules the "sacred touch" as a romantic value. He has said that a painter does not work with Louis Armstrong's trumpet, which is blown with a personal flair. Instead, Fautrier is doing something in painting comparable to what is done by electronic music. He has intentionally duplicated "originals" in series (*les originaux multiples*), throwing on the market a large number of the same "original" so that he can undermine the commercial and artificial value of the unique painting. As he paints his "originals" in series, he alters their details slightly, as if by chance, while the sequence is developing, like the *Otages*, from one work to another. This tactic breaks down the barrier between originals and reproductions. We hear that Fautrier got the idea of doing *originaux multiples* when he sold about two hundred and fifty reproductions of a painting that itself, while exhibited, was unsold and not even asked about. His designs come in the plural, like paper cutouts, as if they were produced on an assembly line. His method of working in series or multiples has been hailed as the beginning of a universal art for the moderns, since it brings into painting what is already available in phonographic recordings, and it has been compared to the change from the manuscript to the book or from the individual theatrical performance to the cinema. Above all Fautrier is attracted to commonplace objects, which for him have a halo of uncertainty. He titles his Glacier series *Glaciers si l'on veut*, and he treats things as if they are things "if you wish."

II

The fascination with the object, the pigment, the operation or execution of painting is best seen in experiments by Dubuffet, who formerly did Kafkaesque views of puppet-like men in city streets. Then he found that "materials are significant in themselves," and embarked on his *art brut*, a revolt against all *grecqueries* and *grandes constructions logiques*. *Vive l'imbecile* is his creed (he agrees with Samuel Beckett), and his work has a grotesque air of comedy that has been compared to *Ubu Roi*. Obviously Dubuffet has a strong sense of the absurd, which he expresses by bruising his pigment, with effects that are droll and at times somber. His exhibit in 1946 at the Drouin Gallery was announced as Mirobolus, Macadam et Cie. Macadam: he is forever making strange *hautes pâtes*, gummy surfaces, from tar and other urban substances. Next he discovered landscape when he spent some months deep in the Sahara, where he saw the forces of geology at work. His series of flattened vertical *Tables* show what challenge Dubuffet found in simple objects after his Sahara journey: they are tables "if you wish," but they are also mountains, escarpments, strata, faultings, rocks, horizons, a disturbing geography from which the figure of man disappears.

Dubuffet considers his paintings an act of sabotage—sabotage, he says in his notes, of the past, of academism, of the Louvre, of the Greeks.* When Dubuffet presents things, one cannot say whether the objects are dematerialized or whether spirit is materialized: there is only the pigment, which is instinctively, directly, selflessly worked; and the painting regresses to a plastic process that is identical with the activity of the painter's hand. Dubuffet's notes and "chats" prove that his intentions tally with Bridgman's in science. Bridgman urged that there be a correspondence between our experience and our description or our idea of it, and that any idea of nature is identical with our operations in examining nature. Dubuffet tells us that no painting is abstract: it is not thought but worked, so that making a painting is like riding a horse. He wants a complete rapport with his material, so he will "falsify nothing and lose nothing." For Dubuffet, everything is landscape, there being a "common rhythm" in things and in the "mental dance that goes on in the mind of man." The texture of his pigment has the prehistoric quality of the earth. When he "finds" the rhythm in matter, then things mutate, and a table changes to a mountain while it is being worked: "les formes affectionnées par la matière vivante sont partout les mêmes"— whether in small things or in the terrain where they belong.

These mutations violently affect the human image wherever it appears in *l'art brut*. When Dubuffet paints man, he wants to restore to him the magic of elemental art: he wishes to "relieve the portrait of all personal traits" and thus escape from "the frenzy of individualism that has ravaged the west for centuries." His brutality is a way of being antipsychological, as he phrases it: he tries to "depersonalize his models" and block all "resemblance." Of his amorphous nude women Dubuffet writes: "My aim was to confer no single figure on this image, and to prevent its having any particular form, so that it might maintain its position as a sort of immaterial concept." There is a "current" set up

* See Appendix, "Excerpts from *Anticultural Positions*, by Jean Dubuffet."

between Dubuffet's mind and the object he regards in its primal anonymity. The painter's hand working the pigment does not refuse objects—instead it makes them portentous, for they ominously and grotesquely magnify their presence as if a certain mana gave them an archaic scale and poise. Although the individual features of man disappear under this brutal caress, man remains as part of a universal geography, taking on a chthonic status.

Dubuffet's painting shows that romantic imperialism is done. The self is no longer able to dominate the world in which it exists. To this extent his painting is not anthropocentric; it represents an obliteration of personality and touch. Yet paradoxically enough after this imperialism has gone, an anthropocentrism persists in a way that can only be called mythical in the sense defined by Ernst Cassirer in his second volume of *The Philosophy of Symbolic Forms.* There Cassirer examines the consciousness of man in relation to his world before the gods have been imaged in an official mythology, before there is any sharp boundary between the self and nature.

In this early phase of consciousness there is no true selfhood because there is no awareness of the limits of the self, of the line between the outer and the inner. It is a state of consciousness when the self seems to dominate the world because the self is actually dominated by things, which it tries to control by means of magic. As Cassirer puts it, there is no "framework of objectivity" into which to fit the things that are vividly intuited. Therefore there are no degrees of reality, since there is no dividing line between perception and representation. The image does not *stand for* the object; it *is* the object. What is perceived is real since man has, as yet, no critical faculty to distinguish between reality and illusion. In this mythical mode of awareness, reality is taken as it is given. Consequently man has no theoretical or rational comprehension of the world of things. He makes, for instance, no distinction between the word and the thing; it exists when it is named. "For mythical thinking all contents crowd together into a single plane of reality."

The result, Cassirer says, is a sense of space and time that is experienced without being rationalized. Since the immediate impression is absolute, the presence of things is very intense, and the image is not measured by anything beyond itself. The object is possessed when it is seen—seen under an "irresistible force with which it impresses itself upon consciousness." Dubuffet has this uncanny sense of the presence of objects, whose appearance is a revelation— a revelation that is entirely uncritical of the various planes of reality, for there is no need to make logical connections, no need to distinguish foreground from background, no perspective or attempt to place the image in any conceptual scheme. The thing represented brings with it a sense of its own causality which Cassirer calls "immediate."

For this reason also the object is capable of metamorphosis, hovering between the subjective and the objective, between illusion and reality, between the dream and the outside world as though it were an apparition seen during a shamanistic trance even while it is overwhelmingly there, in all its purposive and uneasy manifestation, like a sacred thing that cannot be named. The object does not belong in ordered space, though it belongs in a landscape. Its character is ambiguous because it is seen by a self that merges into the world. When Dubuffet says his figures of women are also geological strata or tables, he is invoking a primitive feeling that "Anything can come from anything," for when there are no theoretical laws to isolate cause, relation, succession, there is only the intuition of a thing daemonically apparent to a self that has not withdrawn from the world. There is, to use Cassirer's phrase, no "tragic isolation" of the self. Nor is there any tragic isolation of the object, as there is in painting where things have to be fitted into a nature that is rationally organized, as was the case after the renaissance made laws of perception.

This magical object exists in haptic space: *where* the thing is, is part of its being, and without thinking clearly about its location, the painter offers it as it enters his consciousness, which blurs into the world about him. If there is no distinction between what is represented and what exists, then painting is acting; and painting is identical with the rite of making the painting. Dubuffet's painting is ritual, a manipulation of pigment that is the motion of the painter's hand giving itself over to the activity in nature, from which the self cannot be arbitrarily isolated or, perhaps, even distinguished. The operationalism of Dubuffet's painting is a rite, a participation, a dramatic enactment. His technique is *ensembliste* in a symbolic way.

Robbe-Grillet and the *chosiste* writers have tried to use a sort of operationalism or *ensembliste* technique, leveling man with things, though their art hardly seems mythical. Yet in revolting from psychology, Robbe-Grillet is attentive to "geography." The personality of his characters fuses with their environment. In describing his method, Robbe-Grillet says that the world is neither significant nor absurd—it is simply there; and the cinema is an art, he thinks, able to draw us from the interior of ourselves toward a world where objects are proffered. He would like to be aloof about objects; they should no longer submit to the tyranny of the romantic self, for they are "independent and alien" even while they abide being examined by the mind of man. Therefore we must recognize that the world is no longer our private property, and we must not try to put upon it any "signification" that does not belong to it. The *chosiste* novel rejects the false "depth" of a romantic psychology, which was always trying to read something into things that solidly and immediately exist. The older novel supposed the world hid meanings at its "heart." But the novel should accept the surface of things as reality, not as a mask.

Although Robbe-Grillet works from the outside, there is a strange and perturbing reciprocity between the mental experience of his characters and their world. They make an ensemble. *In the Labyrinth* has this reciprocal texture, for the psychology is wholly dependent upon the scene. As the dazed soldier wanders through the streets of the unfamiliar city, a kind of alternating current is set up between what is outside his mind and what is inside, the two being blurred into a cinematic flow or condition. The development of this novel is a feverish rhythm of recurring images of things, which are also mental states; and this directionless recurrence is much like Fautrier's treatment of objects in a series which can be extended indefinitely. Here as well as in novels like *Jealousy* Robbe-Grillet uses the tropism more ruthlessly than Mme. Sarraute does; he is taking behaviorism to its fictional limit. The psychology in Robbe-Grillet is more brutal than in Proust, who makes sensation lyrical. There is no poetry whatever in Robbe-Grillet, but only the crushing presence of a locale where man happens to be.

The *ensembliste* technique is used again, but less effectively, in Claude Mauriac's novel *Diner en Ville*, where eight characters are grouped into a fictional theory of sets during a few evening hours. The *chosiste* novel readily gives itself to field-effects: witness Michel Butor's *La Modification* (*Second Thoughts*), a study of how the personality of a traveler is displaced into the compartment of the *rapide* bearing him from Paris to Rome. In *L'Emploi du Temps* (*Passing Time*) Butor fuses character with setting more completely.

III

The dehumanizing of art is not, however, so thorough in the *chosiste* novel as it is in Dubuffet's painting, where man becomes anonymous and both painter and figure are absorbed into a turbulent geography that has the quality of mineral or mud. Dubuffet reaches a "zero degree" of painting. It is like the degree of neutrality the modern scientist is seeking when he tries to get outside the systematic logic of an older science that rationalized nature into a coherent system by the scientist's own concepts. The science of the nineteenth century had a false notion of objectivity. Schroedinger tells us why it was false, or unguarded: it was based upon a belief in comprehensibility, a conviction that nature is constructed on rational principles; and it had a hypothesis that the personality of the observer could be excluded from what he observed. If the scientist was "objective," then he could understand the "order" in nature. Thus there entered into science and literature the wholly fictitious detached onlooker—the uninvolved observer who simply "watched" natural law manifest itself. On this hypothetical observer was based a faith that any "experiment" performed impersonally would reveal truth; and Zola's naturalistic novel was an effort to apply this experimental method to art. But Zola's detachment was not only a hypothesis; it was a fraud.

Today the scientist regards the detached observer as a figment, since our mind is part of the process being observed. As Schroedinger puts it, the mind cannot be excluded from the world; the mind *is*, in part, the world, and the sphere of consciousness is included in what is observed. The present question is not one of being "objective"; it is a question of the subject-object relationship. The dilemma of nineteenth-century science was precisely due to the illusion of objectivity: after the world was objectively established as "reality," there seemed to be no place in it for the self. Of course not, the modern scientist replies, because the self is in the world it observes, or at least influences the world it observes. Time and space are not a system independent of the self; nor is matter. The self intrudes into the world of time and space, into geometry, into matter.

Very dramatically Schroedinger remarks that the mind plays a dual role. It is the stage on which events take place, but it is only a part of the stage that it sets. This comes very close to Paul Valéry's notion that poetry is a form of drama in which consciousness watches itself in action. Heisenberg reaffirms this interplay between the mind and the world by saying that at the extreme limits of science we stand face to face with ourselves. "Pure" science is an activity in which the self interacts with the world, and at close quarters. Because of this interacting there is always a zone of indeterminacy—the uncertainty principle. If the mind is in the world, then it is impossible to measure the world unless we get outside the measuring system we use—which, of course, brings us to an impasse. The knower is central in knowledge; that is what scientists once ignored, retreating behind a façade of objectivity.

A certain paradox is implicit in the new science, in anti-painting, in the anti-novel: we find the self by losing the self in things; or, vice versa, we lose the self by finding the self in things. We recover the meaning of things by surrendering to them without supposing we can know them through our own clear ideas of them. Or again, as Zen has it, the thinker is an aspect of what is thought, and the self is an aspect of what it sees. Robbe-Grillet narrows the problem a little further: "Objectivity in the general sense of the term—total impersonality of observation—is all too evidently an illusion. But freedom of observation should be possible." We decide to look at this rather than that. At least we do look at this rather than that. Indeed we must.

Dubuffet has no illusions about objectivity. He is *in* the random texture of his paintings, which have drawn as close as possible to the indeterminate and ambiguous texture that for us is reality. As one of his critics says, after all there is only nature in all her transformations, and his landscapes "boil" with the rhythms in things and in the hand of the painter. Dubuffet's painting has been called a débris left in the arena of chance and necessity—the arena of nature, the nature that is a continuous texture, not a rational structure. It is a nature "without qualities." Yet the "geology of the human" appears in the pressure of the painter's thumb against the pigment, the exertion producing a "residue of the substance of things." The painter gets so far beyond himself in working these elemental textures that there is no difference "between the object and the attention it elicits." In his rapport with the material, the observer fuses with the observed. Dubuffet's art is organic without having the extravagance or the flourish of expressionist painting; this is especially true of the texturologies, which are under-dramatized. By seeming to exclude the human, he finds the human; his mutilation of pigment is a way of committing himself to the indeterminate, a passage where the possible reveals itself as "an unquiet presence of the absurd." It is not heroic art, but humble, comic, self-effacing and self-revealing. If modern science is an account of the relations existing between the mind and nature, Dubuffet's mauled pigments are studies of nature as an operation of man's awareness of nature—or, vice versa, man's awareness as an aspect of nature.

The painter enters the object that elicits his attention and thus loses distance between himself and things, a distance that had always been guarded in the humanistic art coming down to us from the Greeks. Schroedinger has urged science to find a new language that is non-Greek. Dubuffet uses an utterly non-Greek language (unless we grant that Heraclitus spoke such a language). The self no longer dominates the world and gives it "form." Nor is the self excluded, quite artificially, from the nature it is observing. In Dubuffet's "heavy pastes" the self approaches identification with nature. I say approaches, since the troubled movement that still "boils" within the self is impossible to exclude: Dubuffet's painting is agitated even after the image of man has vanished from it. In such painting the self has a radically diminished existence; yet this diminished self—a center of attention—is unquiet. Some of this disturbance is due, also, to nature itself, and is a result of making sensitive observations without attempting to explain away the uncertainty that appears in nature when it is looked at closely.

It is a commonplace to say that modern art is a "retreat from likeness," a withdrawal from the outside world to abstractions invented by the mind. But Dubuffet's retreat from likeness is not an abstraction. Quite the contrary, it is an expression of what Anton Ehrenzweig calls libidinous realism: it loves the world and loses the self in the world without either renouncing the world or seeking to master the world. In fact, this sort of painting could be the most complete surrender to the world that has occurred in Western art; that is to say, the most complete surrender to "reality." It is a far more complete surrender than the realism of the nineteenth century ever made. The so-called realists looked at things, but they did not love things. They wanted to dominate things, as science wanted to.

Ehrenzweig has argued that painting during the renaissance started to "reify" the world and, like science, to cancel out the personality of the artist. It sought to represent the world as it "is" apart from the consciousness of the onlooker. The rigid laws of perspective invented by renaissance painters (who were also mathematicians) were a fiction to make the world look "real," though in truth the laws of perspective were an entirely artificial way of imposing the mind upon things. As painting became progressively "realistic" during the following periods, science was proving the "reality" of the material world governed by "laws" that gave it a false intelligibility. In Ehrenzweig's opinion this process of reification, manifest as realism in art and physical law in science, was actually only a way of repressing man's consciousness—actually only a retreat from responsibility, because art and science alike read into the world, quite dishonestly, the compulsions that existed inside the self. These compulsions, essentially moral, were projected into the natural world as physical laws, the action and reaction of "forces." Thus the self was denied, and alienated from the world. The rational focus of art and science was an excuse for hating the world. The pictures painted by academic formulas in "accurate" perspective were a means of rejecting reality rather than representing it.

Dubuffet has reacted toward a libidinous realism, an appetite for things, and in doing so seems to sabotage art. He has eluded the picture, the motif, and has lost himself in the infra-monde because he loves the actuality and the ambiguity in ordinary objects, which are capable of melting into a universal landscape. Feeling that nature is inscrutable, he has resigned himself to the world as it is, admitting into painting a principle of indeterminacy that is a saving ignorance, humility, and acceptance of man's participation. Pierre Volboudt, writing of Dubuffet, says, "Man must give up the monotone of the 'I.' "

There is a congeniality of spirit between this anti-painting and the science concerned with atomic particles, the stuff of matter. Insofar as the scientist has not been able to observe small particles without affecting them, humanism enters science—man disturbs his environment by his attention. Dubuffet has given up the monotone of the "I" for another monotone, the pigment that is like fiber or lava; and this pigment "ferments" and seems excited by man's consciousness of it.

IV

In taking a libidinous approach to nature, Dubuffet makes almost the sacrifice of the self required by the Buddhist *satori*, the surrender of a man to a flower, a tree, an object seen from the inside. When nature is seen from the inside, man is not necessary, although he is *there*; and the Buddhist paradoxically believes that when one loses the self by seeing a flower from the inside, one finds a self that is not personal but universal. As anti-painter Dubuffet tries to place himself at the interior of rhythms in nature, and to do so he needs to exclude, as far as he can, all reference to himself. When the painter does not strive to bring his own touch and personality to bear upon nature, then he penetrates what is strange to man, entering a primordial landscape that is beyond necessity and chance, since both necessity and chance are notions contrived to make intelligible what is simply and overwhelmingly there.

We may conjecture whether "brutal" painting springs from the same attitudes we find in Zen Buddhism, which has of late strongly attracted Western man by its methods of extinguishing the "I." According to the usual explanation Zen gives a release of consciousness into the universe because the self no longer has a sense of being separate. At the height of Zen meditation our life is not our own, but is extinguished in the world of nature. The Zen doctrine is that by some feat of intellect the mind gets between us and the concrete reality of things, causing us to believe that the self is divided from the rest of creation. Zen is a point of awareness at which the mind breaks down when it passes beyond intellectual constructions and plunges into *samsara,* the cycle of becoming. This release from the self in Zen corresponds in some ways to Dubuffet's reaching a zero point of attention.

Perhaps without knowing it, Robert Linssen, a leading student of Zen, has made a commentary upon the residual selfhood in "brutal" paintings by Dubuffet and others like César Domela. Linssen points out that because our ideas get between us and the world, the only way to enter into close relation with the universe is to immerse the self in all possible points of view, extending as widely as we can our recognition of the universe as it is. This relinquishing of the self by giving up arbitrary points of view is an act of "obedience to things." The scientist would think of this relinquishing as the most attentive degree of observation. If the mind is to regard things without blockage by the self, then it must be freed from the confines of a bi-polar logic which was once so autocratic in morality and in science— "oppositional notions such as good and evil, human and divine, relative and absolute, mobile and immobile." Our interest in Zen is a reaction from a bi-polar theology that has ruled the spiritual life of Western man. One of the compelling themes of bi-polar logic was the opposition of the self to the world, which brought a mistaken sense of individuality. This heightened sense of the self caused only anxiety.

The purpose of Zen is to feel a unity between the self and things, and any intimate submissive contact with things is thwarted by our compulsion to choose; for when we choose "we enclose ourselves within ourselves." According to Zen, giving attention to this rather than to that is a way of excluding reality from our consciousness. Here Zen splits off from the existential notion of man's making his fate through his choices. From a Zen point of view, existential choice is also a trap, a form of egocentricity like a blindness one wills to have. For Zen, the only true choice is to give complete attention to what is: "Satori is the state without choice." It is a state of acceptance. If we are attentive enough to nature, we do not choose: we are chosen rather than choosers. That is, we have extinguished the motives behind our choices.

The inwardness in Zen is not the inwardness of Kierke-gaard, whose compulsion to choose was an extreme romanticism, an assertion of the self in religion, making faith an act of egomania. The deepest Zen experience, the most devout recognition of things, comes after the mind is freed from all preferences. In Linssen's words, we yield the mind to things without having "any particular values" or "points of privilege."

Feeling that a whole landscape reads itself into a simple object, Dubuffet does not have a compulsion to choose, and gives up points of privilege from which preceding painters had looked at the world. Traditionally Western art was imitation (*mimesis*), but by giving up his points of privilege, Dubuffet makes his art participation (*methexis*) as well as imitative in a large sense. His brutal execution is, in Zen phrase, a form of "detachment that is not indifference." It is a "despecializing" of perspective, as is apparent when this painting is compared with cubist perspectives. Dubuffet's "viscous" and mineral landscapes—landscapes "if you wish"—are observations that are motiveless compared with the observation in earlier art. In proportion as this observing is motiveless, freed from special points of view, the painter is freed from all conditioning—from memory, from ideas and theories, from logic, from the despotism of convention. However crude we may think a painting that aspires to be like the surface of a gravel walk, we may see Dubuffet submitting as completely as he can to nature and working as if he believed the Zen axiom that "it is supremely useless to choose anything whatsoever."

This sacrifice of the self in "brutal" art and in Zen implies a belief that "the universe is more important than our recognition of the universe." When we believe this deeply, we lose the self in a silence before things—in Dubuffet's case, before the residual mud or geology. The scientist now takes it for granted that the universe is more important than the observer or his theories. As Linssen notes, the atomic physicist presumes that "the tensorial calculus knows more than the physicist." In this sense the physicist no longer chooses his point of observation; it is chosen for him, and thus he has an attitude toward experiment different from that of the nineteenth-century scientist who set out to prove something. So, also, painting is no longer an act of "imperialism" like romantic art, or even cubism. Dubuffet does not choose his motifs as the older painter did; they are chosen for him by the earth. His canvases know more than he does about nature. The structure of reality flows into them, through his brush, as a current flows through wire. In this way his indiscrimination is an advantage. His art is not "his"; nor can the physicist call the tensorial calculus "his."

When painter or scientist reaches this point in minimizing the self, he gives up the old drama of art and science, and there is a silence of attention comparable to the satori-experience. Satori assumes that if we give ourselves adequately to things, then we do not have to think about them; when we see, we comprehend, and thought exhausts itself. When Dubuffet submerges himself in a pigment like the soil, he exhausts thought about nature. And his texturology is a way of exhausting the technique of painting also in a ritual participation.

Such exhaustion is unlike the classic catharsis at the close of tragedy when with "calm of mind, all passion spent" we were reconciled to what is most human in ourselves and in our human condition. The tragic silence was silence before a vision of man at the highest plateau of his self-sufficiency, a silence before a fate entirely moral in its meaning and therefore saturated by an awareness of a self alien from the inhumanity of the universe. Even at its most atheistic phase, existentialism keeps this tragic tone of man's self-sufficiency, and appeals to man to live by moral instead of natural law. After such tragic actions, man is silent before his own image, not before the world. The silence in Dubuffet is more like the silence in Zen—namely, before a universe that has absorbed man. So, also, the physicist knows that his acceptance of nature must be total, for the "atoms react on the whole universe right up to its ultimate confines," and the relation between things and things, things and the self, is total.

Dubuffet's acceptance, compared with the old tragic acceptance, is total.

V

In science and art this acceptance requires us to refuse mythology. Mythology is not myth, but myth that has been rationalized or verbalized. Mythology is one way of making reality conform to our ideas of reality. The physicist has renounced the mythology he inherited from Greek science, which was homocentric science, extending *Logos* into the cosmos. Dubuffet's anti-painting is mythical; but it is a revolt against mythology in art. To adapt Linssen's words: the mythological is unreal because it is a notion of what should be, created by a mind seeking to confirm the separation between man and the universe. Mythology invents the gods in man's image and puts them on Olympus; it is man's imperialism, born of memory, creeds, rhetoric, shutting us off from what is present, from naked attention to what is *there* before us. In this sense, mythology is a refuge from attention, a way of evading. Mythology can become a cliché in art or science, an orthodox pantheon or theory. The recent quest for myth in literature has often resulted in mere mythologizing, since art cannot fabricate myth. A myth that is consciously intended turns into mythology; and a great deal of Joyce is mythology, not myth. Dubuffet's *Assemblages* erode mythology in favor of myth; they bring before us what in Zen is known as "the necessity of the present." There reality *is*, as the nineteenth-century realists never saw. Having reached this pitch of attention, Dubuffet finds that only geography is necessary. He sees nothing, presents nothing, as he is "supposed" to, and he awaits a revelation of nothing beyond what is there. In a notable phrase Linssen says that "perfect vision is non-expectation." Dubuffet's textures, like the new science, are exercises in non-expectation.

By reaching a state of non-expectation, the scientist guards himself against invoking "laws" of nature that were a sort of mythology. In brutal painting and in advanced physics attention to what is present is more valuable than any of the formulations to be derived from immediate experience. It is easy to overstate a case for the contemporary arts, but it seems that the great contribution of modern painting, or modern science, is a new resignation, a restraint upon the self, depersonalizing art and science as they have never been depersonalized since archaic man accepted the world with a truly mythic consciousness. In making a comparison between satori and the new techniques in physics, Linssen quotes from Gilbert Cahen's *Les Conquêtes de la Pensée Scientifique* to the effect that the scientist has done all he can to disregard the personal equation: "Faced with the fact, he wants to be invisible, impersonal, nonexistent." Yet the modern physicist is wiser than the nineteenth-century scientist who presumed he could be wholly objective; for he knows he is the center of the attention he brings to bear upon facts. As a center of attention, he knows that "the scale of observation creates the phenomena." Thus the observer is like a lens that distorts. His observations are inalienably *his* observations; but he must, as far as he can, depersonalize his system of observation, yielding himself to the evidence and allowing himself to be chosen by his experiment. To be sure that he is chosen and not the chooser, the experimenter must "give up his well-anchored habits of thought, euclidean geometry, three-dimensional reasoning, constancy of the mass. . . . This catharsis, this successive abandonment of our familiar modes of apprehension of the universe, seems an inexorable law in the development of modern theories in physics." The inexorable law is not in nature but is the need to resign ourselves to reality.

By disdaining mythologies, the scientist comes to nature in a mood of non-expectation that is truly Olympian when it is compared with the provincialism of nineteenth-century science. Cahen hopes he can question the universe knowing that he is devoted to seeing things as they are: "The denudation of phenomena, when faced with the immediate content of our perceptions, presents two characteristics. . . . On the one hand, this process reveals an identity of essence between the intellect and the universe. On the other hand, this content is progressively emptying itself of its apparent substance: matter itself tends to be but an empty form, a field of action of the structural properties of our mind, that is to say, of something immaterial. We will express thus, and in the most extreme manner, the ultimate tendency of science: the reduction of reality to the void. This void is not not-being, nullity. It is, on the contrary, the most complete being possible since it potentially contains the universe." We recall that Dubuffet wanted to confer on his nude women no particular form; they maintain themselves as "a sort of immaterial concept."

Dubuffet's *Assemblages* are abstractions; they are also residues left after the painter has dismissed all his expectations about reality and "suspended thought." Concerning his paintings that have been called "philosophic," Dubuffet has written, "I have intended to stress the material of objects, their *presence*." But their presence is "immaterial" because they belong to a realm of "universal rhythms, systems where the movement of matter coincides with the dance of man's mind." Anything that looks human in his figures, he protests, is only "grafted" on: their textures may evoke a notion of human flesh, but never of flesh alone— also notions of bark, rocks, dunes, leaves, or the soil. He will not accept a "heresy of separateness." What he paints is particular and material; but like atomic activity it reaches the limits of the universe. Falsifying nothing and losing nothing, he has absorbed the painter in his painting. By evading the self he has extended cubist methods beyond their classic phase, during which the mind of the painter exercised a powerful and intelligent tyranny over the object.

By attending to the object, Dubuffet has, paradoxically, extinguished the object, which recedes toward absence.

Art and science have been carried along together on the main currents of modern thought, as Marcel Brion insists, even if their similar direction was not intended: "In most cases the artists had no personal acquaintance with the books or philosophical theories that had changed the direction of thought, but they were influenced by them because they lived in the climate determined by that thought, because, by virtue of their sensibility, they are interpreters of their epoch . . ."

VI

For all their accommodating the psychology of character to the scene in which the character appears, writers like Robbe-Grillet have not subtracted the self in quite the same way as the "brutal" painters who have a sense of the disturbances in the indeterminate world of matter. Sartre has this sense more strongly than the *chosistes*. Yet in Robbe-Grillet the law of entropy works, for the character is absorbed into a field, though here again the absorption is more complete in painting, where the object is liquidated amid apparently random movements that are only probabilities or possibilities. As for poetry, Eliot's later verse shows a nearly oriental desire to cancel the self, and reaches a level of abstraction common in painting where, in Eliot's phrase, the detail of the pattern is movement.

The loss of the object in painting was accompanied by a loss of the object in Eliot's poetry. In the 1920's Eliot used very concrete images, sharply faceted, like the objects analyzed in cubist painting. Then in *Ash Wednesday* he turned from the actualities of time and place, and from the infirm glory of nature, to a more abstract and contemplative language adopted from Dante and the Orient: "Or say that the end precedes the beginning, and all is always now." It seems as if Eliot, along with scientists and painters, was convinced that behind objects and events there are only abstract relations (where nature was "there is nothing again"). Thus Eliot's verse moves with the prevailing trend toward nonobjective art, which preceded anti-painting.

While Eliot was losing the object, he was also trying to deliver poetry from the burden of the romantic self. Like T. E. Hulme, he wanted poetry to be impersonal. Yet in spite of Eliot's much-quoted opinion that poetry ought to be an escape from personality, Wallace Stevens was the one who probably liberated modern poetry more completely from the romantic self. Stevens said that romantic poetry was merely a "minor wish-fulfillment" closer to sentimentality than to liberty of imagination because it made literature a reflection of life, whereas life is a reflection of literature. That is, literature frees us from actuality, and from the pressures of emotion, by establishing an abstract mental geography, which is the extreme feat of the poetic imagination. This geography exists "in the crystal atmospheres of the mind"—what Stevens calls "the poetry of thought." To exist in this geography, the poet must abandon all romantic gestures and center his vision on a supreme fiction, "which you know to be a fiction, there being nothing else." Eliot wanted to make poetry impersonal by exploiting a medium, not emotions. Stevens proposed something more radical, perhaps, in saying that "the poetry of thought should be the supreme poetry," delivering us from the "corruption of reality" by "the momentum of the mind." The poet must get beyond romantic melodrama by a pure construct that has some similarity to abstract painting by Mondrian, filtering emotions and perceptions through an idea of an order. The poem that remains after such filtering is, in Stevens' phrase, "the form of life," Projection C, the scheme of relations between thing and idea, or the apparition of So-and-So reclining on her couch as if suspended:

> . . . To get at the thing
> Without gestures is to get at it as
> Idea. She floats in the contention, the flux
> Between the thing as idea and
> The idea as thing.

To see her thus is to cleanse the imagination of romantic sentiment, along with the weight of actualities.

And while the object was being lost in painting and poetry, the self was becoming increasingly anonymous in a society where the individual seemed important only as a statistical item. In spite of Freud's therapy for the ills of the private self, the individual was disappearing behind graphs plotted by human engineers. If poetry was not impersonal enough to suit Eliot, there was more than enough impersonality in society.

The sign of this devouring anonymity was Kafka's hero, known merely as K, the nameless victim of bureaucracy and lineal descendant of the underground man. Kafka's nameless person is modern man oppressed by his own identity. In that textbook of spiritual misery, the little diary called *He*, Kafka writes, "Sometimes in his arrogance he has more anxiety for the world than for himself." The self inside this vanishing hero knows it is a self largely because it is "a vindication of nothingness, a justification of non-entity, a touch of animation which he wanted to lend to non-entity." Kafka's personage describes his life as an "astonishment at the tremendous complex" into which he is thrown. He has a paralyzing "fear of one's responsibility for things." A Marxist critic, Georges Lukacs, has complained that Kafka destroys the image of the person by making all reality subjective. Kafka, he says, reduced experience to fragments, dissolved character into fantasy, and offered us nothing but an abstraction. To be sure, Kafka's characters are in flight, and their existence is a long nightmare. But it is not true that they have lost touch with the human condition, for

Kafka's fictions demonstrate his own maxim that we can reach the truth about ourselves only by exaggerating. At grotesque extremes Kafka represents the experience of those who live in an age of concentration camps. Along with Samuel Beckett, Kafka pushes literature beyond the safety zone; and his short stories, especially, resemble the koan exercises in Zen, intended to have a shock effect, as if they were parodies of textbook logic. A novel like *The Trial* is not fantasy; it is a caricature of conventional fiction, and as such is a variety of anti-novel. And in common with all caricature, it has its own kind of abstraction distorting what is normal.

It is quite unlike the other abstraction to be seen in the Stijl movement and painting by Mondrian, whose art is a *démondinasation* of a very ascetic and fragile variety. This abstraction is closer to a theory of relativity that is able to abbreviate reality into the equation $E = mc^2$. Enraptured by clarity, Mondrian approaches pure thought, a luminous geometry, and he subtracts the self by severely reducing consciousness to a prismatic play of the mind. His is a tradition of abstraction essentially different from anything in Kafka, Dubuffet, or Beckett, who lose the self without emptying art of an existential content. To resist being oppressed by things, Mondrian wanted to abandon the concrete, to pay homage to his immaculate conceptions. In his thirst for ideal forms he is curiously sympathetic to Plato, who turned his back on the muddled world of things. Mondrian's painting is an act of iconoclasm; it dares to purge the comic and tragic, and it disregards large areas of sensation. After making these exclusions, Mondrian is able to erect constructions that are like a scholasticism of the engineering mind. Though the Stijl group wanted to discipline art closely by scientific theory, such painting adheres to the formulas rather than to the spirit of modern science, which may be better represented by the less spartan performance of Dubuffet or of Jackson Pollock.

One is doubtful whether the art of De Stijl reflects very fully the thought of scientists like Whitehead or Heisenberg. Instead, it is a technological vision, or the reverie of a geometer. The technologist plans intelligently and designs efficiently, whereas our speculative science does not plan its way beyond the existential. The scientific imagination has thrived of late upon the enigma of the concrete—what Whitehead called the ultimate matters of fact lying at the heart of the atom and reality. Mondrian approaches reality from the remote limits of mathematics; he conceives the delicate ratio, isolates it, and presents it with a decision that is inspired. Heisenberg and the atomic physicists study the submicroscopic probabilities of an activity that verges off toward the random. What is most real in Dubuffet's painting is its grotesque fabric of hazard, an instabilty at the core of things, a caricature of structure.

Something like this hazard is everywhere in modern experience. It is a hazard that frightened Kafka's personages, who shrank from the uncertain by disappearing, by being inconspicuous and as anonymous as they could. Their worried desire for anonymity brings us full circle from the exuberant anonymity of Walt Whitman, who did not face any such hazard and who also desired to lose his identity in a quite different way and for a quite different reason. Whitman hoped to expand himself to embrace everyone and everything: "I am large, I contain multitudes," he announced in *Song of Myself*. With nearly epic heroism he made himself prodigious by being divinely average and amplifying the individual to democratic infinities. Whitman's verse was likewise a brand of anti-poetry. His scuttling of literature was done by some of the tactics common among the "beats," whose subversion is yet another venture in losing the self.

SEVEN

Beat Subversion

I

The European subversion of literature and art we have been describing is essentially anti-romantic, and amounts to a desperate attempt to suggest the inauthenticity of our lives. One sign of its desperation is its belief that "meaning begins to be dated." For this reason it prefers silence, which Mauriac says is a suicidal impulse in literature. The scuttling of literature by American "beats" is also said to be a form of silence—though in print, at least, the beats have been torrentially communicative. Everyone seems agreed that Walt Whitman's lavishly ordinary self is reincarnated in Henry Miller, the spiritual forefather of Kerouac, who in turn seems to be a father-image for Gregory Corso, Allen Ginsberg, Lawrence Ferlinghetti, and the younger beats who publish. Undeniably the abundance of Whitman resembles the abundance of Kerouac and beats who have used literature as a means of making their headlong and uninterrupted confessions. This unchecked loquacity is sufficient proof that these beats belong to a romantic tradition never averse to exhibitionism and the exploitation of a personality. There are, of course, silent beats, whose ancestor is Henry David Thoreau, not Walt Whitman.

The beats who make their books confessional and descend from Whitman must not be confused with European subversives like Nathalie Sarraute, Ionesco, Robbe-Grillet, or Samuel Beckett. For one thing, these continental subversives are far more deeply committed to the philosophic adventures of our age, and their philosophic adventures are more sophisticated than the beat taste for Zen. In brief, saboteurs abroad are more intelligent, more informed. Besides, they have an intense interest in literary technique, and each has based his work on a thoroughgoing critique of method. Even if they did not wish to say anything, these continental writers would be important for their experiments, which are often knowing to the point of being overcultivated. It seems equally improper to associate our beats with British angry young men, who are not very angry and not a group anyhow, and who have made minor contributions of a rather regional sort. The beats thus seem to be particularly American. Possibly there is a connection between the American hipster and French writers like Céline and Genet, for some of our beat colonies have settled at the brink of the lower depths where rebellion goes over to crime. Céline and Genet, however, are quite self-conscious about literary method, and their work is an act of aesthetic as well as moral defiance. Norman Mailer has said that hip means "violence, new hysteria, confusion and rebellion." All these are in Céline and in Genet, who asserts, "Je suis ivre de vie, de violence, de désespoir." But in addition to désespoir, and beyond his interest in what is forbidden, Genet is able to treat sadism, perversion, crime in novels or dramas where fantasy modifies autobiography. All in all,

the American subversion seems naïve, and once again there
is a lag between European and American writing, causing
our beat poetry, especially, to fall back upon the outworn
devices of Dada. The American writer is not at the moment
avant-garde, as he was in the twenties when Hemingway
and Faulkner began.

Instead, Kerouac and Ginsberg regress to some of the
romantic methods that derive from Whitman, perhaps by
way of Thomas Wolfe and Henry Miller, who says he loves
rebels and failures. An expatriate and professional outsider,
Miller illustrates the exceptional status of Americans in the
present world—he is fed up with our prosperity, and refuses
to allow *Time* magazine to run his emotional life. In one
of his best works, *The Air-Conditioned Nightmare,* Miller
rejected the fatness of our pursy days, and decided to quit,
to disaffiliate, to get along without "the garbage of material-
ism," to give himself to a new hedonism that was not yet
"cool," but, instead, a kind of "random bohemianism."
From the first, Miller's writing was drenched with an ebul-
lient optimism, a Whitmanesque cordiality, which has been
lifted by his followers to the plane of the holy. The sham-
bling geniality of Miller's books is expressed in a passage
from *Tropic of Capricorn:* "Everything is sentient, even
at the lowest stage of consciousness. Once this fact is grasped
there can be no more despair. At the very bottom of the
ladder, chez the spermatozoa, there is the same condition
of bliss as at the top, chez God. God is the summation of
all the spermatozoa come to full consciousness." The great
chain of being *chez* the U.S.A.

So Miller lets the tide of bliss wash over him, as Whitman
did, in sprawling confessions that are too literary to be anti-
literature and too slovenly to be literature. Miller may claim
to be "the germ of a new insanity, a freak dressed in intelligible language, a sob that is buried like a splinter in
the quick of the soul." Yet the insanity is often bathos; it
is not the absurdism of Kafka or Ionesco, much less Beckett.

The splinter in Miller's soul is hardly a mortal wound. In *Tropic of Cancer* appears his creed: he wants to get off the gold standard of literature; he hopes to reach a literary stratosphere "in the grip of delirium." The delirium is a way of abandoning himself to sentimentality. He has a bland confidence that he is "inoculated against every disease, every calamity, every sorrow and misery." That is to say, he is hopelessly American. (On January 8, 1961, the New York *Times* ran a Sunday article on the United States with the title "Why Are We Blessed?" Among the letters this queasy interrogation inspired, not one countered by a question "But Are We Blessed?" Instead, the replies printed seemed to assume that we are.) To be inoculated against every sorrow and misery is either innocence or self-indulgence— or simply Rotarian. It is like the Hollywood cemeteries where organ music is piped into tombs to solace the bereaved.

The second generation of beats are able to write only in superlatives. As Kerouac says with damning complacency: "So there's nothing to get excited about. Beat comes out, actually, of old American whoopee." Live your lives out? "Naw, *love* your lives out." Everything is beatific; everything is holy. "Who knows, my God," Kerouac goes on, "but that the universe is not one vast sea of compassion actually, the veritable holy honey, beneath all this show of personality and cruelty." I suppose the worst one can say of this is that it is self-satisfied, immature, and ignorant as only Americans can be ignorant nowadays.

At the same time one must admit that the beats are authentically modern in their wish to get out from under the burden of our apparatus. Ginsberg reports that he has seen the best minds of his generation numbed and destroyed. Paul Goodman has documented this opinion in *Growing Up Absurd*. The beats want to resign, in reaction against Korea and the cobalt bomb. They ask, "Whose world is coming to an end?" The question is well put. Yet in a sense their world is, along with the world of *Time* magazine, because they too are a symptom of an affluent American society that has produced them by satiating them. They are witness that we do grow up absurd. They are uniquely American because they reject a society that makes more and more useless goods which more and more thought-less persons are persuaded to buy.

They feel disgusted, not anguished. Their disgust takes the form of a marriage to heroin or peyote: "Catatonia here we come." The beats are wise enough to see that terms like insanity, psychosis, and a-social conduct are only soph-isms useful to those whose emotional life is run by *Time*, and who in effect are far madder than the beats. As they say, madness is a dated notion, like an Ibsen play. Kerouac writes in *On the Road:* "The only people for me are the mad ones, the ones who are mad to live, mad to talk, mad to be saved, desirous of everything at the same time, the ones who never yawn or say a commonplace thing, but burn, burn, burn like fabulous yellow roman candles exploding like spiders across the stars and in the middle you see the blue centerlight pop and everybody goes 'Awww.'" One way to sustain this euphoria is to take peyote. The need for *another* intoxication is very American, and the fun of always saying "Awww" is like the exhilaration of buying product after product you don't need or want. These high spirits can be supported in an economy of abundance, where even madness is a holiday.

Yet after a fashion the Dharma Bums mark a return to the monastic life of Thoreau, a disburdening of the excess we have learned to call necessity or prosperity. In an over-stuffed society they refuse to corrupt themselves in the usual way by consuming what they don't want anyhow—"refrig-erators, TV sets, cars, at least new fancy cars, certain hair oils and deodorants and general junk you finally always see a week later in the garbage." However, this disburdening is unlike Thoreau's ascetic retreat; for Thoreau lived alone, and without the emotional abundance that inspires the beat to dig everything. Kerouac says the beats are "a swinging group of new American men intent on joy." The beat renounces one kind of excess to give himself to another. When interviewed, Kerouac announced, "We love everything, Billy Graham, the Big Ten, rock and roll, Zen, apple pie, Eisenhower—we dig it all. We're in the vanguard of the new religion."

Their new religion has a Zen vocabulary; but they have changed the austere Buddhist doctrine of no-mind to a subterranean innocence or a gargantuan appetite for whatever happens. How far does Zen serve the purpose Theosophy once served when Helen Blavatsky sought to get beyond the individual self by "becoming one with the Infinite" and proclaimed that "every man has his paradise around him"? The Theosophists believed in a "universal Divine Principle" absorbing the false personality by saturating it with the higher self, Atma, neither your spirit nor mine, but ours.

Jazz is the vernacular of the beat communion, in which beatitude does not take the form of silence before nothingness, but of feeling joy in groups. The ecstasy is democratic, like Whitman's. Jack Green admits that his peyote personality "may have been affected by group suggestion." The hipster does not, he says, feel any need to talk, but above all he wants a sense of togetherness; and his simplification of language is a way of reassuring his fellow hipster that "I'm with you, I've got you." The need for communion sends the beats barreling from coast to coast—driving "cross-country seventy-two hours to find out if I had a vision or you had a vision or he had a vision. . . ." Barreling across country is one more American luxury—an emotional luxury in place of the chrome-plated luxuries that have been dropped. At its worst this beatific communion is banality, a plunge into the commonplace, which may be called holy but which lacks anything that might rightly be considered mysterious.

II

There is a threshold below which the peyote personality of the beat darkens into anguish, and where hipsterism touches the realm of crime. This is the quasi-tragic level of beat revolt against our phony morality. It is the level at which Genet writes, knowing that he has given himself over to *le mal*—evil. Ironically enough, the crossing of the border into criminality is required to give hipsterism an ethical quality necessary to literature. So too, the author's sense of evil, or his pride in being delinquent, gives novels by Céline and Genet a note of authentic modern experience.

It is a note heard in Jack Gelber's *The Connection*, a drama that functions well outside the "normal," like *Journey to the End of Night*. The derelicts in Gelber's play, waiting for their fix, are moral desperadoes, who are perhaps the only kind of tragic heroes available at the moment in a world of atomic bombs and germ warfare. Instead of Kerouac's euphoria, there is a recognition that runs like a chorus through this play: "That's the way it is. That's the way it really is." These Negroes and whites are waiting for a fix to forget, because, as Sam says, "I can't stand the silence any more." When Jaybird brings them the heroin, he mutters that after all the changes are played, we're back where we started. "We end in a vacuum." One of the junkies says he is fed up with everything, and is waiting for a little hope: "A fix to remember, to be sad, to be happy, to be, to be." The connection is coming—always coming—"but so is education." Their overdose of heroin takes them to the thin line where they swing between life and death: what else "can make so much of passing out?" They do not fear the silence of passing out, the silence of nothingness. They fear the silence of their daily routine. So they wait: "We have waited before." They wait for death; but that doesn't matter either.

I do not know whether Gelber was imitating Samuel Beckett; but all this could have been said in any of Beckett's anti-novels, which go beyond the point of no return. Gelber's play takes place in a sordid hipster setting. The characters, however, are not merely hipsters. They are carried along on the main current of despair and weariness running powerfully through continental writing. Their predicament causes a poet like Robert Lowell to speak of "the horror of the lost self." This is the predicament faced by the nameless heroes in Samuel Beckett, who shows better than anyone else how lost the modern self can be.

The Anonymous Self:
A Defensive Humanism

I

Beckett's novels are studies in the extreme attrition of personality, an advanced stage of entropy in the self. One British reviewer has noticed that the theme of all these novels was stated in 1931 in Beckett's book on Proust; there he spoke of "the only world that has reality and significance, the world of our own latent consciousness." In fact, it is almost a misnomer to talk of character in Beckett's novels, for the consciousness of the central figure is vestigial, a vague residue of man's anxieties. *The Unnamable* is a commentary by the obliterated figure called "I" who stands patiently at the threshold of an existence fringing off into silence—the silence Hamlet feared might be troubled by bad dreams. This is an "end game" in literature, the anti-novel in one of its most random and submerged forms. Yet it is not random in meaning, for there lingers during this retreat a shadow of a personality that Beckett wants to erase before he falls back into nothingness. Beckett writes variations upon the old question whether to be or not. Now the answer is plain: it is better not to be. Perhaps we cannot be, anyway. This seems to be implied at the close of *Comment C'est*, when the creature flat on his belly in the mud suspects that Pim, Krim, and Kram weren't ever there. All the heroes in Beckett exist with a minimal presence. The great trouble is to diminish even this minimal presence. It has been said that these anonymous heroes are reincarnations of Charlie Chaplin. Very likely, except that the slapstick is gone, and only the pathos and dejection are left. Chaplin was a sort of high-spirited Kafka. Vladimir and Estragon exist in a scene where there is no longer even a legend of the Castle.

"How can one be sure in such darkness?" That is Beckett's first question, which Kafka might have asked. But these novels are not surrealist dreams, like Kafka's. They are inquisitions into our existence as Heidegger sees our existence: a self emerging from nothingness, but only discontinuously, and with great uncertainty. Beckett's anti-hero is one to whom things bafflingly happen; his consciousness has shrunk to only a point at which events become dimly apparent. By a logic of contradiction, he exists only as evidence of his own insignificance, and his experience is a way of raising doubts about the reality of his being. "Is it possible certain things change on their passage through me, in a way they can't prevent?" asks The Unnamable. This is similar to the question Dubuffet asked of his paintings, which are manifestations of *hasard*; and their strangeness is due to what is *insolite*, the unwonted. The existence of Beckett's hero is possible, not actual, and he is always on the point of returning to nothing.

He is at the opposite pole from the romantic hero who willed his world into being. He exists beyond the safety zone—but at the opposite direction from the romantic hero.

By his willful existence the romantic hero put everything else in danger; everything else puts Beckett's hero in danger. So he spends his life sucking stones. Pressed back beyond extremes of caution, he speculates, "Things are to be expected. The best is not to decide anything, in this connection, in advance. If a thing turns up, for some reason or another, take it into consideration." This reads nearly like a parody of the Zen surrender to things—perhaps Zen with an infusion of despair. The critics say that Dubuffet's paintings abolish the need for man as an independent spectator. Beckett's heroes are unnecessary, even as spectators.

The Unnamable is quite uncertain where the margin of a self is: "But it's not I, it's not I, where am I, what am I doing, all this time, as if that mattered." What occurs to him—or in him, or through him—does not seem to be his: "He has no story, he hasn't been in story, it's not certain, he's in his own story, unimaginable, unspeakable, that doesn't matter, the attempt must be made, in the old stories incomprehensibly mine, to find his, it must be there somewhere, it must have been mine, before being his." This anti-hero is alien from himself, from events that apparently happen to him. But he is not the others either; and inexplicably he is different from events that are in his story. The others seem to be indispensable to his presence. The Unnamable gives existentialism another turn, for although the others are involved in his being, he cannot commit himself to them. As for making any choice—that would be a romantic gesture. Since Beckett's nameless character is mostly acted upon and cannot "make" his own fate, existentialism is put into reverse. *They* are not *he*. Yet they affect him. "Do they believe it is I who am speaking? That's theirs too. To make me believe I have an ego all my own, and can speak of it, as they of theirs. Another trap to snap me up among the living. It's how to fall into it they can't have explained to me sufficiently."

We cannot speak of action in Beckett's novels, for the hero is fixed in what might be called a condition, which in some ways resembles the continuous texture in "brutal" painting. The condition is not, however, inert; that is the puzzle. Inertia is to be expected; what affects Beckett's characters is some disorder in their condition, a disturbance that causes not irritation but malaise, bafflement, or depression. The malaise is suppressed so far below the level of pain, it does not even quicken the pulse. Thomas Mann called life a fever in matter. The fever runs very low in Beckett; but it is chronic, and its causes are endemic in the obscure situation around The Unnamable. The difficulty is to find what this fever feeds itself on, so great is the debility of the self. The inviolable precinct of the self seems to be its stupidity, which is an instrument of resistance that insures its survival at this minimal level: "They'll never get the better of my stupidity." Beckett's anti-hero exists *because* he is muddled, because he is ignorant.

"My inability to absorb, my genius for forgetting, are more than they reckoned with. Dear incomprehension, it's thanks to you I'll be myself, in the end. Nothing will remain of all the lies they have glutted me with." They have taught him to count, even to reason; and he does not deny that some of this rubbish is convenient on occasion. He will have greater confidence if he asks no more questions. "To tell the truth, let us be honest at least," says The Unnamable, "it is some considerable time now since I last knew what I was talking about. . . . I'll fix their gibberish for them. I never understood a word of it in any case, not a word of the stories it spews."

This comforting stupidity does not always help, since at moments he has compulsions he cannot rid himself of; and though these compulsions are undirected, they interfere with his staying quietly in his corner. He has a need to utter something—it is never clear what, and it does not matter what. "I have no voice and must speak, that is all I know."

It would be simpler if the voice were surely his; but there are doubts about this, too: ". . . of that I must speak, with this voice that is not mine, but can only be mine, since there is no one but me, or if there are others, to whom it might belong, they have never come near me." If the voice is not his, at least there is a point of view behind what is said; but no one is there to take this point of view. The monotone of the "I" is barely audible, and consciousness is suspended in some state where it seems foreign to man's nature. There is a locus of attention; but it is unassigned. Just as man has disappeared within Dubuffet's geological pigments, man is at the point of disappearing—with great uneasiness and anxiety—as Beckett's nameless persons interrogate themselves to search out some center for their awareness. They can say nothing certain. Their sense of being confused is too remote.

The rest is silence. Eliot retreated into the silence of a Chinese jar moving in its stillness. Mondrian reached a silence where art becomes superfluous, a quietness of clear thought, which is an untroubled order of absolute geometry, a dialectic of color and line above suspicion. Feeling that we live in a climate where all is suspicious, Mme. Sarraute listens to our babble and learns that it is our way of avoiding silence. Beckett's silence is a hazard, a darkness we face without hope or insight. We ache for this silence, but cannot make our quietus. The Unnamable has been almost able to shuffle off this mortal coil, but has no more confidence than Hamlet that ceasing to be will suffice. In fact, one interpretation of Beckett's novel is that The Unnamable is speaking from the after-world. If this is a permissible reading of the book, one can only say that Hamlet's father is better off in his purgatorial fires than Beckett's ghost is in his limbo, where he has neither peace nor punishment, foreknowledge nor memory. The existence of The Unnamable seems, rather, to be a prolonged graveyard scene, but without the comfort of any sane Horatio to remind him that imagination must not consider too curiously how we return to the dust, and also without the blunt logic of the gravediggers.

The Unnamable does not come Hamlet-like from Wittenberg to the rotten state of things; but he does have thoughts beyond the reaches of his soul—thoughts like Hamlet's bad dreams. He has listened to their words, words, words; he suspects they dare not be silent long lest their fabrications collapse into the gulf he feels himself leaning over. He fears these gulfs as Hamlet fears the horizons he scans. But like Kafka's heroes, he yearns to plunge into them: "I dread these gulfs they all bend over, straining their ears for the murmur of a man. It isn't silence, it's pitfalls, into which nothing would please me better than to fall, with the little cry that might be taken for human, like a wounded wistiti, the first and last, and vanish for good and all, having squeaked." Eliot guessed we would end going round the prickly pear; but the whimper of his hollow men was a human sound compared to the cry Beckett's figure utters.

At the end of this end game he does not know whether he has ever lived—he really has no opinion on the subject. However that may be, he will go silent for good, since that's not prohibited. Beckett's anti-self is a travesty of the existential notion of engagement. To be engaged, one must have a self to engage. Beckett is not entirely sure there is this self. He wonders. Molloy suspects that if he goes on long enough calling it his life, he'll end by believing it: "It's the principle of advertising." The peace he wants will come to him, he thinks, when he does not want to know anything, when he is beyond knowing anything. Malone dies feeling "very grey." He has an impression that he emits grey. "What tedium," he sighs. By reducing his painting to monochrome, Dubuffet implies that man is unnecessary, that the human is only an aspect of what happens. This monochromatic texture is disturbed by currents rising from some deep undertow; they are like the eddies in consciousness drifting along the pages of Beckett's novels, which are also monochromatic. Dubuffet's willingness to use a pigment having the fluid and uniform texture of mud corresponds, it may be, to Molloy's opinion that living is like moving through muck: "It's a change of muck. And if all muck is the same muck that doesn't matter, it's good to have a change of muck." Beckett's subtracting from the existential self is so complete that only minus values remain. For this novelist man is no longer the sole hero, but only the center for what he sees; and from a zero point of attention he looks across into the realm of the indeterminate, where man vanishes into the infra-world.

In all his anti-novels Beckett repeats his theme. After finding that nothing is more real than nothing, Malone dies alone, suffering at first more, then presently less—"without drawing any conclusions." He could, if he wished, die now; but it is well not to rush things. As he lies waiting to die tepidly, feeling that his feet are somewhere out there beyond the range of a telescope, his one care is to guard against "throes." But the throes come, as a vestige of existence that cannot, evidently, be subtracted. Perhaps, he decides, he has lived after all without knowing it.

While Watt lived in Mr. Knott's house, he learned to "accept that nothing had happened, learned to bear it, and even, in a shy way, to like it." But sadly enough, "then it was too late." Molloy explains that if he has not mentioned everything in its proper place, "it is because you cannot mention everything in its proper place, you must choose between the things not worth mentioning and those even less so." This is why he spends his days sucking stones. Hamlet had at least his roles to play, his drama to act, while he stood at the edge of nothingness; he had a theatrical chance to die with a flourish like a sweet prince. All was ill about Hamlet's heart, but he went to his death believing there is providence in a sparrow's fall. The readiness was all. The readiness: this is Beckett's note—except that the readiness is a dismal wish to have done. As Molloy says, "That's what counts, to have done."

II

Beckett's nihilism is a last phase of anti-literature, and *The Unnamable* brings up to date a tradition that began in the eighteenth century with *Rameau's Nephew*, then went on through Dostoevsky and Gide and Kafka. Beckett's wish to extinguish the self is not the romantic nihilism of Nietzsche or the terrorists or other nineteenth-century heroes for whom suicide was an ultimate affirmation of the self. Paradoxically enough, the romantic nihilist made the self an absolute by destroying the self. With Beckett the affirmation is gone; but the paradox remains, for after the self has shriveled, the human remains—in some unlocalized area of perception or response. To repeat: we have an existence, however unwillingly, after we have lost an identity; and we do not seem to be able to diminish this existence below a certain point. Beckett's hero has no voice, but he must speak. Or as The Unnamable says, nothing troubles him; yet he is troubled.

His nothingness strangely keeps its tinge of pain, doubt, solitude, despair. He has dim recognitions, intimations that are his, though they cannot give him a secure sense of selfhood. Beckett speaks across huge voids of despondency. The nineteenth-century existentialists said that we do not live until we reach a "boundary situation" where the self is in great peril; we have to "stake" everything as we stand there alone. The boundary where Kierkegaard stood divided the finite from the infinite, the self from God, and at this frontier the knight of faith felt the "endless yawning difference" between human and divine. The boundary is still there although the self has been almost effaced, but the confronting of man and the infinite is no longer heroic because our self is enfeebled and because our sense of identity has withdrawn deeply into what is only a point of attention from which we watch. It must be *our* attention. It must be our awareness, however dim, or our malaise. If this is really our situation, Kierkegaard looks very romantic indeed with his challenge to the single one and his core of passionate inwardness, a feat of defiance by which one laid claim to selfhood. The passionate inwardness is done; yet a disturbed and disturbing zone of existence persists, minimal though it be. It must be man's, irreducibly.

This is a humanism so gloomily qualified I have called it defensive. It lessens itself to our reading of reality after man has been removed from the center of what he reads. The reading is done so hesitantly in Beckett, the residual consciousness is so thoroughly defensive, one is reluctant to use the term humanism, although one must admit that Beckett's blurred personalities touch us to the quick. So far as "brutal" painting is involved, the case is a little different since the zero degree of humanism in Dubuffet's art might better be called reflexive than defensive. As Pierre Volboudt, one of Dubuffet's critics, points out, after the "brutal" painter has removed man from the center of his representations, a miracle occurs in spite of the renunciation of the "I": for reality succumbs to its image, and the painted work triumphs, as it always did, over actuality. The representation remains after the painter is negated. Thus Dubuffet's anti-painting proves that art is a unique human privilege even after the self has diminished to a locus of attention. It also proves that man's consciousness is an inherent aspect of the reality to which he submits his consciousness, although this consciousness may be far displaced from the center.

For this reason, presumably, Sartre and Camus are convinced that man has a "privileged metaphysical position." That is to say, as long as man is aware of his existence as being absurd, thwarted, blocked, or irrelevant, a variety of humanism persists, simply through man's awareness of his plight. It may persist only as evidence that our perception distorts what we perceive. It may simply be a consciousness that man is helpless, that humanism in the old sense is no longer valid. The very awareness of the untenability of a bygone humanism is itself a humanistic verdict. Our consciousness that we have been ousted from the center, or that the world is but a figment of our consciousness, or that our consciousness is but a figment in the world, is a recognition of the inalienability of the self. As Richard Coe has said, the only remaining meaningful act for many modern artists is a discovery that the world is meaningless. There is meaning in Ionesco's putting before us the "meaningless mirror of a meaningless world." Thus in *The Rhinoceros* Bérenger remarks how he isn't sure he is himself because life is an abnormal business. In the same way Genet proposes in *The Balcony* that the "dead" are those who do not take part in "the illusion that is life." If living be an illusion, or a delusion, we are the locus for the supposition that living is an illusion. In short, however unwilling we may be to do so, we seem forced to base our strange and negative humanism on Bridgman's premise that there is meaning in a meaningless statement. To be conscious of the meaninglessness is to have a metaphysical position that is privileged; and we do not seem able to abandon that position.

Defeated as he is, Beckett implies in his anti-novels that we cannot, in spite of everything, annihilate selfhood—there is a self that wishes to die quietly. The most despairing passage in Beckett is a triumph of artistic comprehension or perception: The Unnamable says, "Come come, a little coöperation please, finish dying, it's the least you might do, after all the trouble they've taken to bring you to life. The worst is over. You've been sufficiently assassinated, sufficiently suicided, to be able now to stand on your own feet, like a big boy. . . . They have put you on the right road, led you by the hand to the very brink of the precipice, now it's up to you, with an unassisted last step, to show them your gratitude." After the classic disasters are done, we still have a need for tragic resignation.

Beckett's minimal humanism is the theme of *Waiting for Godot,* a play about which there is great disagreement. It is evident that Vladimir and Estragon are waiting for a deity. But does he appear? Pozzo, who does appear, would be, in the first act, the terrible Old-Testament God, the tyrant-divinity; and in the second act Pozzo would be a New-Testament God, manifesting himself as injured, cruci-fied, helpless, offered up for the sins of the world, as much a victim as those who await him—and he is wholly depend-ent upon the support of some institution like the Church. Beckett seems to be posing the question whether Pozzo in either form is an acceptable god; or whether man can have any valid notion of god. If Lucky is the Jew or the Christian, then the situation is indeed desperate. And is the boy the evangelist of an Unknown God, who never appears, who disdains to appear, whom man cannot know, who is ir-relevant anyway, whom we are too stupid to worship? The minimal humanism of this play is centered in Vladimir, who has trouble with his head, and who knows there is "Nothing to be done." After Pozzo has come and gone, after the boy makes a couple of speeches that sound like a parody of T. S. Eliot's liturgical verse, Vladimir is still there, having got used to the muck as he goes along.

This decomposition of the human along with the per-sistent residue of selfhood is the theme, also, of Ionesco's play *The Rhinoceros,* which translates Beckett (and per-haps Camus?) into popular theater. The ordinary citizen Bérenger finds people in his town growing horns and thick green skins: they have caught the rhino virus, and one by one Bérenger's friends "go over" as the metamorphosis of man to beast becomes commonplace. One of his friends says, "We must consider what is normal and average. Where does the abnormal begin? You must learn to be detached. I'm only trying to be realistic and look at facts objectively. We must move with the times. What's wrong with being a rhino? I'm all for change." The townsfolk agree that hu-

manity is out of date; it's all washed up. Besides, rhinos
have energy; and if they are going to be a majority, "we
must understand how their minds work." One of Bérenger's
friends is a logician, and he is able to meet the rhino crisis
by using a little method: "All cats die, Socrates is dead.
Therefore Socrates is a cat." Will Bérenger also consider that
"a cat has four paws; my dog has four paws; therefore my
dog is a cat." Since Bérenger cannot conquer his own stupidity, he is unable to go over, and at the end of the play
remains stubbornly human. A great deal of this harks back
to Kafka's story *Metamorphosis*, with Gregor Samsa waking
one morning to find himself changed into a roach. But the
difference from Kafka is striking, for Gregor the roach is
alone. At the close of Ionesco's piece, Bérenger the man is
alone.

In *The Rhinoceros* Ionesco has used many of the tricks
of conventional theater; at least it is not an anti-play like
Waiting for Godot. There Vladimir roughly corresponds to
Bérenger, both characters retaining, after human nature has
been severely discounted, a nondeductible selfhood. Vladimir's humanity is more equivocal, more worn away, than
Bérenger's, and much harder to bear. Throughout, Beckett
is morose, and uses a more menacing tone than Ionesco.
Yet *The Rhinoceros* bandies many of the themes we have
been following—the peril in the average, the breakdown of
logic, the need to find or maintain a self in an age that
seems determined to shed, if it can, individuality, freedom,
and responsibility. These are themes Albert Camus was
concerned with, and Camus probably leaned as far as Beckett over the gulf to which we have been led by the hand.

III

Camus' response was not Beckett's, nor Ionesco's; and
Camus cannot, in spite of *The Stranger,* be easily bracketed
with writers of anti-literature. For one thing, since his pri-

mary interest was not literature but social and moral issues, he may have his long-range importance mainly through *The Rebel*, which may remain as one of the best accounts of the dangers of romantic heroism, and of its various ways of going to the brink. Notwithstanding the attacks that are made on his work, Camus was as deeply involved as anyone in our modern dilemmas, including the dilemma of the modern self. What Camus wrote is hard to get into balance because without being a writer of anti-literature, he dealt with situations I have been calling post-existential. In his particular way he corroborates what Elizabeth Bowen once said in lecturing: a novelist should not be too far in advance of his day. Holding to a very modest notion of the self, Camus did not take his position in the extreme *avant-garde*, yet was equipped to meet the difficulties of holding *avant-garde* salients.

As for his modest position: I refuse to seek reassurance in Camus' book that is usually taken to be reassuring—*The Myth of Sisyphus*. It is too stoic, too devoted to a heroism that is quasi-classic. Sisyphus—who is nobody but modern man placed in a very strong light—is inspiring as he rolls the great stone to the top only to see it fall back; he rolls it up again and finds meaning in the very struggle. This view of life is braced with tragic courage, but for that reason is somewhat inaccessible to us, since we are, after all, taking part in an end game with Vladimir and Malone. It would be quite unfair to say that Sisyphus has the stupid confidence of Browning and the romantics who urged us to strive, never to grudge the throe. Nevertheless the figure of Sisyphus speaks an old tragic humanism that is a little out of date when we read Beckett or look at Dubuffet. In presenting Sisyphus, Camus is invoking an attitude expressed in one of Bertrand Russell's essays written in 1918, "A Free Man's Worship." Russell is more melodramatic than Camus; the significant thing is that both writers, in spite of themselves surely, are forced into a posture not very different, in essence, from the romantic posture Shelley had at the close of *Prometheus Unbound*—that is, man must, in a hostile world, create his own values, and devote himself to them. Man against the universe, in short. Russell urges us to admit that the world was not made for us; and we must go on from this despair to a tragic confidence in ideals we must erect unaided. Camus would be embarrassed to use the rhetoric of Russell's closing passage (it is only decent to add that Russell is probably embarrassed by having written it), the passage in which man's life is said to be brief and doomed in a universe blind to good and evil and moving to destruction in its relentless course; so before the blow falls Man must be "proudly defiant of the irresistible forces that tolerate, for a moment, his knowledge and his condemnation, to sustain alone, a weary but unyielding Atlas, the world that his own ideals have fashioned despite the trampling march of unconscious power."

Sartre would probably be as resentful as Camus to have his existential position compared to Russell's position at the close of "A Free Man's Worship." But for the sake of defining Camus' humanism, it is necessary to digress for a moment to note how this morality of resistance becomes a little stagy not only in Sisyphus but in Sartre's plays. The heroism of Orestes in *The Flies* is almost as embarrassing as the heroism in Russell's essay: once freedom lights its beacon in man's heart, the gods are impotent. Orestes feels that freedom has crashed down on him like a thunderbolt; after murdering his mother, his hands are red, but he is free—beyond anguish, remorse, or despair. The heavier the burden, the more it pleases him. (Sisyphus is somewhat less pleased.) Only the cowardly murderer feels remorse. Orestes is a successful Raskolnikov: he moves to the far side of crime, proudly defiant. This is, of course, only one half of Sartre's existentialism, for when one chooses, one chooses for mankind. Yet Sartre is often betrayed by an existential heroism, the heroism that still places man's destiny within himself. Man surges up in the world, defines himself, and has sole responsibility for his existence. True (in a sense); but, after reading Beckett or Sarraute, somewhat lofty perhaps.

Fortunately *The Myth of Sisyphus* does not represent in full the humanism in Camus. Other passages are more relevant to our need for an unheroic heroism, passages where Camus tells us we are all together in a trap we have made for ourselves because we are all guilty: actually and individually guilty. To this degree we share a communal personality. When I choose wrongly, I choose for you. This is orthodox existentialism, and brings in an anti-romantic principle, for romanticism in discovering the self gave the self an irresponsible freedom, the liberty of man against the world, alone. Camus is wiser. He knows what I owe to the others. He also knows what the others owe to me. He knows that in every modern heroism there must be a degree of self-obliteration. He has placed the existential self, with its passion for authenticity, into a context of the anonymous, the context in which Beckett's Unnamable appears so faintly. The boundary situation in Camus is impressively there, but ill defined. Sartre defines it sharply by Orestes' crime.

In an early fiction like *The Stranger* Camus writes his own anti-novel having an anti-hero. Meursault behaves with an automatism that sends him to the brink of the absurd. His personality is strictly conditioned—he murders (unlike Sartre's Orestes) because the sun is hot, and his finger mechanically pulls the trigger. The act is—and is not—his. Social codes mean nothing to him; they are not his either. He is guilty and not guilty. He is a sub-rebel, existing in a condition that is amnesic or numbed. He has a self that is alien to himself; and his experience is so detached from himself as to be schizoid or catatonic. The others affect him not at all: not Marie, not his mother, not the judge. He is disengaged.

In *The Fall* Camus presents the other extreme—a parody of the existential notion of engagement with the others. It is also a parody of our "social" point of view, our belief that morality is merely a group norm. Clamence is the ultimate man without qualities: he has no friends, only accomplices, and he has abdicated from all obligations by displacing responsibility into society. He is a specialist in making us all feel answerable and, therefore, guilty; he corrupts us all by the power given us today—the social conscience. Clamence knows that his guilt is contagious *because* he is typical. Because we are foul, he is foul; and because he is foul, I am foul. His sin destroys my innocence. We fall together. *Our* fall precedes *his* fall; but he drags me down with him. Clamence is a modern satan who desecrates our Eden, who plunges us into a communal guilt, a guilt that is anonymous but mortal. Clamence puts romanticism into reverse, for we are all free to be guilty. He levels us by exploiting the existential theme that we are all together in the field of human experience, that I cannot isolate my self from your self, that we are all accountable. But Clamence also passes judgment on us, the judgment of the pseudo-penitent who infects us with his infection. He spreads the plague.

However the answer to Clamence had already been given by Dr. Rieux and Tarrou in Oran, where the infection was as common as it was in Paris or Amsterdam. *The Plague* cannot be called an anti-novel; perhaps it is not a novel, but a tract upon our condition. Tarrou is a Meursault who has survived the guillotine; he passed beyond the accepted "order of things" when he saw his father, a judge, send a wretched little criminal to execution; it was the act of a man without qualities, a functionary of the law who was not concerned with a human being, but only with the professional abstraction called "justice" to which an abstraction called "the defendant" was subject. This is the disease that breaks out in Oran, the contagion of our anonymity, which dehumanizes our existence. Tarrou helps Dr.

Rieux organize sanitary squads. Neither knows why he helps others. Rieux can find no better name for it than "common decency." He feels that this is an absurd expression. But at least it sterilizes him against thinking of himself as heroic. Rieux apologizes to Tarrou: "Heroism and sanctity don't really appeal to me, I imagine. What interests me is being a man." Rieux takes up a position between Sisyphus and Sartre's Orestes. He favors an anti-heroic notion of heroism that has something in common with the irreducible selfhood Vladimir cannot cast off while he is waiting for Godot.

The anonymous humanism toward which Camus was always working is more acceptably phrased in his "Reflections on the Guillotine," which seems to me to summarize what he most wanted to say about the modern self. It is in the form of an indictment, running as follows: "The disease of Europe is to believe in nothing, and to claim to know everything." If we believe in nothing, then all executioners are humanists, since they cannot be wrong—a form of sentimentalism that is cowardice, not charity, because it ends by justifying whatever is worst in the world. "If everything is blessed, then the slave camps are blessed." (It is a sentence our beats have often ignored.) In other words, if we are all guilty, nobody is guilty.

"Nevertheless," Camus adds, "I do not believe there is no responsibility in this world." Here is Camus' commentary on the experiences of Meursault, the anti-hero who at the hour of his death looks up at the vast indifferent sky with a sense that he gives himself up to the inevitable, that our fate is more than ever impersonal, that the self is negligible after all. This is Meursault's comfort, his act of half-tragic resignation before he dies. Like Beckett's hero he leans over the abyss of nothingness, though he has the advantage of a numbness Molloy and Malone cannot induce in themselves. When Camus says we are individually responsible for the disasters around us, disasters that have numbed us or caused us to explain them away as history, he takes up again the theme of Robert Musil's novel, or anti-novel. He speaks as unromantically as Rubashov in Koestler's *Darkness at Noon,* when the former Stalinist functionary discovers he is personally liable for the deaths of Arlova and little Loewy.

Camus' stand is not very far from Martin Buber, whose brand of existentialism mediates between the anarchic individuality of Kierkegaard with his "single one" and the obliteration of the self in social psychology. Buber holds two theses that appear to be contradictory: Individuality is what makes each one different from the others; and individuality is gained only by entering into relations with others. Buber starts from the premise "In the beginning is relation." One of the relations that has become increasingly oppressive is the "augmentation of the world of It." Along with Musil and Camus he thinks this dominance of the It is injurious. Yet it need not be if the I can enter into relation with the It; and when the I brings its consciousness to bear upon the It, then the It is amenable to an interrogation more subtle than the interrogation by the older science, which established no relation between the mind and the world. "Without It, man cannot live. But he who lives with It alone is not a man." The I-Thou relation is more appropriate between man and man; and through this most precious of relations Buber hopes to make existence a form of coexistence. As Buber listens to existence, he waits for something other than an echo of the "I." There should not be an echo, but a resonance between the I, the Others, and the It. Buber rejects the imperialism of the self still apparent in Sartre's Orestes.

Camus has this abiding sense that the self must come into relation with the others. What is perhaps unique about Camus is that he plunged deeply into the destructive element without losing his sense that the self is, absurdly enough, anonymous but accountable. He passes judgment on us together and separately; we are guilty in common and we are guilty alone. He will not have us fall into the abyss with a little human squeak. Without approving of the romantic self or any existential freedom that begins on the far side of crime, Camus went the length of urging the artist to create dangerously—which, doubtless, was his way of agreeing with Ionesco that the writer must pass beyond the safety zone. But to create dangerously, or to live defiantly, was not, for Camus, to sanction nihilism—"I am tired of nihilism," he said in one of his last lectures. Camus looked upon romanticism as an irresponsible kind of freedom. He was seeking another notion of freedom and responsibility. It is a notion that comes only when one is aware that he lives with others, but faces the others alone. Camus works his own variation on a theme once set by André Malraux, who in *Le Temps du Mépris* said "It is hard to be a man." Camus answers that it is impossible not to be a man.

▭ ▭ ▭ ▭ ▭ ▭ ▭ ▭ ▭ ▭ ▭ ▭ ▭ ▭

Note on "Decision, Order, and Time in Human Affairs," by G. L. S. Shackle

A reconsideration of the whole problem of the self and a deterministic social science is found in G. L. S. Shackle's book *Decision, Order, and Time in Human Affairs* (1961), which is nothing less than an existentialist economics, differing from classical economics in rejecting the notion of economic law as absolute. "Conventional economics," says Shackle, "is not about choice, but about acting according to necessity." Yet conventional economics insists that the basis of economic law is the choice each man freely makes for himself. "Choice in such a theory is empty, and conventional economics should abandon the word." Antieconomics replaces economics.

Shackle takes nondeterminism as a premise to human history. His re-examination of economic theory parallels Lupasco's re-examination of the laws of logic and the scientist's re-examination of the iron laws of nature. By way of coping with C. P. Snow's dilemma, Shackle holds that decision is possible, real, and effective in history, and that decision creates history itself. As he defines it, decision is a choice made in view of bounded uncertainties, a choice at a moment of crisis he calls the "solitary present" because it is unlike any other moment that has been or ever will be— "the solitary moment of actuality."

A choice that is made creates something new, initiating original impulses in the wave-pattern of history. If the laws of history are determinate and absolute, then no choice is possible. Precisely because the laws of history are not determinate, but only a range of bounded uncertainties, decision is real; and every decision changes the situation. Each decision is an experiment in human experience that cannot be repeated since it is "self-destructive," arising from a moment and a situation that are unique. No decision, then, is "empty." Consequently history is a "one-way traffic" that cannot be interpreted by "laws." The laws of history are useful only if decisions that have been made are real; but if a decision is real, then it is unique, an upsurge from the "solitary present." Thus there is no ground for a predictive law of history, no genuine choice ever being predetermined or "given."

Shackle's book is a scrutiny by a statistician of the laws of large numbers as applied to society, and in effect rejects human engineering as a science capable of dealing with man. There is a great difference, he points out, between a controlled laboratory experiment, which can be repeated, and any experiment involving persons who make decisions, or choices, moment by moment as if each decision were inspired. An outside observer can calculate the course of history by a scheme; but the man who makes history by choosing cannot know in advance what he is creating when he chooses. The calculator uses what Shackle calls an exterior dynamics; but the one who chooses is freed from calculations by an internal dynamics involving personal impulses belonging to the single mind and the single moment. In short, history cannot really be understood by a detached observer to whom all dates are equally valid as they occur along the course of extended time or a "calendar axis." A real choice or decision is a "cut" into time; a decision does not work in extended time, which is like a mathematical concept.

Existential history is not only unpredictable: it depends upon contingencies and develops within the limits of the "uncertainty variable," which Shackle tries to formulate statistically by degrees of expectation. Here again, the expectation is that our expectation will change. Shackle has tried to bring into political science a new "calculus of human conduct" entirely unlike the Benthamite hedonistic calculus, which was mechanical and exterior. Instead, Shackle's existential economics hinges on choices made in the face of bounded uncertainties; or, if we may use the term, he has invoked an existential statistics.

By arguing that choice and creative freedom are not illusory, he has also introduced a certain humanism into the so-called laws of economics. As Shackle puts it, we cannot overcome our sense of freedom, and a predestined economics is something different from the "explosion of essential novelty" inherent in acts and giving a personal meaning to the thought and feeling that inspired them. Economics, he thinks, needs to be brought back to "the nature of that actuality which we know by conscious experience and which is contained within a solitary present moment."

Excerpts from "Anticultural Positions,"
by Jean Dubuffet

In his lecture given at The Arts Club of Chicago in December, 1951, Jean Dubuffet talked on "Anticultural Positions." The following passages are excerpts from that lecture, here reproduced with the gracious consent of M. Dubuffet and The Arts Club of Chicago.

I think, not only in the arts, but also in many other fields, an important change is taking place, now, in our time, in the frame of mind of many persons.

It seems to me that certain values, which had been considered for a long time as very certain and beyond discussion, begin now to appear doubtful, and even quite false, to many persons. And that, on the other hand, other values, which were neglected, or held in contempt, or even quite unknown, begin to appear of great worth.

I have the impression that a complete liquidation of all the ways of thinking, whose sum constituted what has been called humanism and has been fundamental for our culture since the Renaissance, is now taking place, or, at least, going to take place soon.

I think the increasing knowledge of the thinking of so called primitive peoples, during the past fifty years, has contributed a great deal to this change, and especially the acquaintance with works of art made by those peoples, which have much surprised and interested the occidental public.

It seems to me that especially many persons begin to ask themselves if the Occident has not many very important things to learn from these savages. May be, in many cases, their solutions and their ways of doing, which first appeared to us very rough, are more clever than ours. It may be ours are the rough ones. It may be refinement, cerebrations, depth of mind, are on their side, and not on ours.

Personally, I believe very much in values of savagery; I mean: instinct, passion, mood, violence, madness.

Now I must say I don't mean to say that the Occident lacks these savage values. On the contrary! But I think that the values held up by our culture don't correspond to the real frame of mind of the Occident. I think that the culture of the Occident is a coat which does not fit him; which, in any case, doesn't fit him any more. I think this culture is very much like a dead language, without anything in common with the language spoken in the street. This culture drifts further and further from daily life. It is confined to certain small and dead circles, as a culture of mandarins. It no longer has real and living roots.

For myself, I aim for an art which would be in immediate connection with daily life, an art which would start from this daily life and which would be a very direct and very sincere expression of our real life and our real moods.

I am going to enumerate several points, concerning the occidental culture, with which I don't agree.

One of the principal characteristics of Western culture is the belief that the nature of man is very different from the nature of other beings of the world. Custom has it that man cannot be identified, or compared in the least, with elements such as winds, trees, rivers—except humorously, and for poetic rhetorical figures.

The Western man has, at last, a great contempt for trees and rivers, and hates to be like them.

On the contrary, the so called primitive man loves and admires trees and rivers, and has a great pleasure to be like them. He believes in a real similitude between man and trees and rivers. He has a very strong sense of continuity of all things, and especially between man and the rest of the world. Those primitive societies have surely much more respect than Western man for every being of the world; they have a feeling that the man is not the owner of the beings, but only one of them among the others.

My second point of disagreement with occidental culture is the following one. Western man believes that the things he thinks exist outside exactly in the same way he thinks of them. He is convinced that the shape of the world is the same shape as his reason. He believes very strongly the basis of his reason is well founded, and especially the basis of his logic.

But the primitive man has rather an idea of weakness of reason and logic, and believes rather in other ways of getting knowledge of things. That is why he has so much esteem and so much admiration for the states of mind which we call madness. I must declare I have a great interest for madness; and I am convinced art has much to do with madness.

Now, third point. I want to talk about the great respect occidental culture has for elaborated ideas. I don't regard elaborated ideas as the best part of human function. I think ideas are rather a weakened rung in the ladder of mental process: something like a landing where the mental processes become impoverished, like an outside crust caused by cooling.

Ideas are like steam condensed into water by touching the level of reason and logic.

I don't think the greatest value of mental function is to be found at this landing of ideas; and it is not at this landing that it interests me. I aim rather to capture the thought at a point of its development prior to this landing of elaborated ideas.

The whole art, the whole literature and the whole philosophy of the Occident, rest on the landing of elaborated ideas. But my own art, and my own philosophy, lean entirely on stages more underground. I try always to catch the mental process at the deeper point of its roots, where, I am sure, the sap is much richer.

Now, fourth. Occidental culture is very fond of analysis, and I have no taste for analysis, and no confidence in it. One thinks everything can be known by way of dismantling it or dissecting it into all its parts, and studying separately each of these parts.

My own feeling is quite different. I am more disposed, on the contrary, to always recompose things. As soon as an object has been cut only into two parts, I have the impression it is lost for my study, I am further removed from this object instead of being nearer to it.

I have a very strong feeling that the sum of the parts does not equal the whole.

My inclination leads me, when I want to see something really well, to regard it with its surroundings, whole. If I want to know this pencil on the table, I don't look straight on the pencil, I look on the middle of the room, trying to include in my glance as many objects as possible.

If there is a tree in the country, I don't bring it into my laboratory to look at it under my microscope, because I think the wind which blows through its leaves is absolutely necessary for the knowledge of the tree and cannot be separated from it. Also the birds which are in the branches, and even the song of these birds. My turn of mind is to join always more things surrounding the tree, and further, always more of the things which surround the things which surround the tree.

I have been a long time on this point, because I think this turn of mind is an important factor of the aspect of my art.

The fifth point, now, is that our culture is based on an enormous confidence in the language—and especially the written language; and belief in its ability to translate and elaborate thought. That appears to me a misapprehension. I have the impression, language is a rough, very rough stenography, a system of algebraic signs, very rudimentary, which impairs thought instead of helping it. Speech is more concrete, animated by the sound of the voice, intonations, a cough, and even making a face and mimicry, and it seems to me more effective. Written language seems to me a bad instrument. As an instrument of expression, it seems to deliver only a dead remnant of thought, more or less as clinkers from the fire. As an instrument of elaboration, it seems to overload thought and falsify it.

I believe (and here I am in accord with the so called primitive civilizations) that painting is more concrete than the written word, and is a much more rich instrument than it for the expression and elaboration of thought.

I have just said, what interests me, in thought, is not the instant of transformation into formal ideas, but the moments preceding that.

My paintings can be regarded as a tentative language fitting for these areas of thought.

I come to my sixth and last point, and I intend now to speak of the notion of beauty adopted by occidental culture.

I want to begin by telling you how my own conception differs from the usual one.

The latter believes that there are beautiful objects and ugly objects, beautiful persons and ugly persons, beautiful places and ugly places, and so forth.

Not I. I believe beauty is nowhere. I consider this notion of beauty as completely false. I refuse absolutely to assent to this idea that there are ugly persons and ugly objects. This idea is for me stifling and revolting.

I think the Greeks are the ones, first, to purport that certain objects are more beautiful than others.

The so called savage nations don't believe in that at all. They don't understand when you speak to them of beauty.

This is the reason one calls them savage. The Western man gives the name of savage to one who doesn't understand that beautiful things and ugly things exist, and who doesn't care for that at all.

What is strange is that, for centuries and centuries, and still now more than ever, the men of the Occident dispute which are the beautiful things and which are the ugly ones. All are certain that beauty exists without doubt, but one cannot find two who agree about the objects which are endowed. And from one century to the next, it changes. The occidental culture declares beautiful, in each century, what it declared ugly in the preceding one.

The rationalization of that is that beauty exists surely, but it is hidden from view for many persons. To perceive beauty requires a certain special sense, and most people have not this sense.

One believes also it is possible to develop this sense, by doing exercises, and even to make it appear in persons who are not gifted with this sense. There are schools for that.

The teacher, in these schools, states to his pupils that there is, without doubt, a beauty of things, but he has to add that people dispute which things are endowed with that, and have so far never succeeded in establishing it firmly. He invites his pupils to examine the question in their turn, and so, from generation to generation, the dispute continues.

This idea of beauty is however one of the things our culture prizes most, and it is customary to consider this belief in beauty, and the respect for this beauty, as the ultimate justification of Western civilization, and the principle of civilization is involved with this notion of beauty.

I find this idea of beauty a meager and not very ingenious invention, and especially not very encouraging for man . . . . I find even this idea that the world we live in is made up of ninety percent ugly things and ugly places, while things and places endowed with beauty are very rare and very difficult to meet, I must say, I find this idea not very exciting. . . .

I just said, and I repeat now, painting is, in my opinion, a language more rich than that of words. So it is quite useless to look for rationalizations in art.

Painting is a language much more immediate, and, at the same time, much more charged with meaning. Painting operates through signs which are not abstract and incorporal like words. The signs of painting are much closer to the objects themselves. Further, painting manipulates materials which are themselves living substances. That is why painting allows one to go much further than words do, in approaching things and conjuring them.

Painting can also, and it is very remarkable, conjure things more or less, as wanted. I mean: with more or less presence. That is to say: at different stages between being and not being.

At last, painting can conjure things not isolated, but linked to all that surrounds them: a great many things simultaneously. . . .

I am indebted to the following writers, whose books or articles I have either quoted directly or used as background.

Berger, Klaus: *Géricault and His Work*, 1955

Bridgman, Percy W.: *The Logic of Modern Physics*, 1927, 1960
"Science and Common Sense," in *Great Essays by Nobel Prize Winners*, ed. Leo Hamalian and Edmund L. Volpe, 1960
The Way Things Are, 1959

Brion, Marcel, ed.: *Art Since 1945*, 1958

Bronowski, J.: *The Common Sense of Science*, 1960

Bucarelli, Palma: *Jean Fautrier*, 1960

Burtt, E. A.: *Metaphysical Foundations of Modern Science*, 1954

Cassirer, Ernst: *The Philosophy of Symbolic Forms*—Volume II, Mythical Thought, 1955

Coe, Richard N.: *Eugène Ionesco*, 1961

Cohn, Robert G.: *The Writer's Way in France*, 1960

De Sua, Frank: "Consistency and Completeness—A Résumé," *American Mathematical Monthly*, LXIII, no. 5, May, 1956

De Sua, Frank: "Metamathematics: A Non-Technical Exposition," *American Scientist*, XLII, no. 3, July, 1954

Dubuffet, Jean: *L'Art Brut Préferé aux Arts Culturels*, 1949
Prospectus aux Amateurs de Tout Genre, 1946

Ehrenzweig, Anton: *The Psycho-Analysis of Artistic Vision and Hearing*, 1953

Fitzsimmons, James: "Jean Dubuffet," *Quadrum*, no. 4, 1957

Fromm, Erich: *The Sane Society*, 1955
Zen Buddhism and Psychoanalysis, 1960

Giraud, Raymond: *The Unheroic Hero*, 1957

Grenier, Jean: *Essais sur la Peinture Contemporaine*, 1959

Guicharnaud, Jacques and Beckelman, June: *Modern French Theatre*, 1961

Haftmann, Werner: "On the Content of Contemporary Art," *Quadrum*, no. 7, 1959

Heidegger, Martin: *Existence and Being*, ed. Werner Brock, 1949

Heisenberg, Werner: *The Physicist's Conception of Nature*, 1955-58
Physics and Philosophy, 1958

Humphreys, Christmas: *Zen Buddhism*, 1958

Jaffé, H. L. C.: *De Stijl*, 1956

Jammer, Max: *Concepts of Force*, 1957

Jaspers, Karl: *Man in the Modern Age*, 1957

Langan, Thomas: *The Meaning of Heidegger*, 1959

Limbour, Georges: *Tableau Bon Levain à Vous de Cuire la Pâte*, 1954

Linssen, Robert: *Living Zen*, trans. D. Abrahams-Curiel, 1958

Lukacs, Georges: *La Signification Présente du Réalisme Critique*, 1960

Lupasco, Stéphane: *Logique et Contradiction*, 1947

Mauriac, Claude: *The New Literature*, 1959

Novotny, Fritz: *Painting and Sculpture in Europe, 1780 to 1880*, 1960

Polanyi, Michael: *Personal Knowledge*, 1958

Ponente, Nello, ed.: *Modern Painting*, 1960

Ragon, Michel: *L'Aventure de l'Art Abstrait*, 1956
Dubuffet, 1959, 1960
Fautrier, 1957

Rudrauf, Lucien: *Eugène Delacroix et le Problème du Romantisme Artistique,* 1942

Schroedinger, Erwin: *What Is Life?,* 1956

Steiner, George: "Retreat from the Word," *Kenyon Review,* Spring, 1961

Tapié, Michel: *Esthétique en Devenir,* 1956
    Mirobolus et Cie., 1946
    Observations, ed. Paul and Esther Jenkins, 1956

Volboudt, Pierre: *Les Assemblages de Jean Dubuffet,* 1958, 1959

Watts, Alan: *This Is It,* 1960

ABOUT THE AUTHOR

WYLIE SYPHER is professor of English, dean of the
graduate division and chairman of the division of lan-
guage, literature and arts at Simmons College in Boston.
Born in Mount Kisco, New York, Mr. Sypher was grad-
uated from Amherst College, received master's degrees
from Tufts College and from Harvard, and a Ph.D. from
Harvard. He has taught summers at the University of
Wisconsin, the University of Minnesota, and at the Bread
Loaf School of English, and twice has been awarded a
Guggenheim fellowship for research in the theory of fine
arts and literature. His book, *Four Stages of Renaissance
Style*, published in 1955, has become an influential work
on its subject. His other books include *Enlightened Eng-
land*, *Guinea's Captive Kings*, and *Rococo to Cubism in
Art and Literature*.